MW00466042

The Cat That Ate the Cannoli

Rabbi Barbara Aiello

The Cat That Ate the Cannoli

Tales of the Hidden Jews of Southern Italy

Hadassa Word Press

Impressum / Imprint
Bibliografische Information der Deutschen Nationalbibliothek: Die Deutsche Nationalbibliothek verzeichnet diese Publikation in der Deutschen Nationalbibliografie; detaillierte bibliografische Daten sind im Internet über http://dnb.d-nb.de abrufbar.
Alle in diesem Buch genannten Marken und Produktnamen unterliegen warenzeichen-, marken- oder patentrechtlichem Schutz bzw. sind Warenzeichen oder eingetragene Warenzeichen der jeweiligen Inhaber. Die Wiedergabe von Marken, Produktnamen, Gebrauchsnamen, Handelsnamen, Warenbezeichnungen u.s.w. in diesem Werk berechtigt auch ohne besondere Kennzeichnung nicht zu der Annahme, dass solche Namen im Sinne der Warenzeichen- und Markenschutzgesetzgebung als frei zu betrachten wären und daher von jedermann benutzt werden dürften.

Bibliographic information published by the Deutsche Nationalbibliothek: The Deutsche Nationalbibliothek lists this publication in the Deutsche Nationalbibliografie; detailed bibliographic data are available in the Internet at http://dnb.d-nb.de.
Any brand names and product names mentioned in this book are subject to trademark, brand or patent protection and are trademarks or registered trademarks of their respective holders. The use of brand names, product names, common names, trade names, product descriptions etc. even without a particular marking in this work is in no way to be construed to mean that such names may be regarded as unrestricted in respect of trademark and brand protection legislation and could thus be used by anyone.

Coverbild / Cover image: www.ingimage.com

Verlag / Publisher:
Hadassa Word Press
ist ein Imprint der / is a trademark of
OmniScriptum GmbH & Co. KG
Bahnhofstraße 28, 66111 Saarbrücken, Deutschland / Germany
Email: info@hadassa-wp.com

Herstellung: siehe letzte Seite /
Printed at: see last page
ISBN: 978-3-639-79405-2

Copyright © 2015 OmniScriptum GmbH & Co. KG
Alle Rechte vorbehalten. / All rights reserved. Saarbrücken 2015

for

Angela Yael and her son Alessandro Yosef

B'nei Anusim who became the first members

of Synagogue Ner Tamid del Sud

Serrastretta, Italy

Table of Contents

These articles originally appeared in the Times of Israel as Blog Posts. They are used with permission.

My Grandmother's Candelabra

Shining a Bright Light on Secret Jewish Traditions

For thousands of Italians who live in the southern Italian region of Calabria, the island of Sicily and the Aeolian Island chain, connecting family traditions with an ancient Jewish heritage can be little more than a lucky guess. But as *b'nei anusim* (those who were forced into Christian conversion during Inquisition times) continue to search for their lost and hidden Jewish roots, one ritual item, the Shabbat candelabra offers an important clue.

For years I believed that the triple candelabra that was one of our family heirlooms was a lovely artifact of inconsequential meaning. Later as I began a search of our family's *anusim* roots, I discovered that this three-branched candelabra was a special part of the family Shabbat table.

As the founder of the *B'nei Anusim* movement in Calabria and Sicily, it has been more than a decade since I began asking questions about our lost traditions. Over the years the answers I gleaned from families living in ancient mountain villages astounded me. One elderly woman told me, "The middle candle served as *"nu sustiagnu rande"*, Italian dialect for "the helping candle". And then, as she demonstrated this with her own three-branched candelabra, I noticed that just as Jews use the shamus candle to light the eight candles on the Chanukah menorah, an Italian shamus candle was used to light the two candles for Shabbat.

The peacock motif found on my Aiello - Scalise family candelabra offers another Jewish clue. For the crypto-Jews of Calabria, the peacock was an important element in Jewish design. Originating with the Kabbalists, the Jewish mystics of medieval times, it is the male peacock's special feather configuration that is reminiscent of the Kabbalistic "third eye". This symbol connects with the message of Shabbat by reminding us that with the "third eye" we can see into a person's soul and thus bring peace to the world.

Families in Serrastretta, the tiny village where we have organized "Ner Tamid del Sud", the first active synagogue in Calabria in 500 years since Inquisition times, recall the three branched candelabra at their own Friday evening dinner table. Some have memories of a beautiful ritual where the matron of the house first lit the middle shamus candle, removed it and then passed it to the youngest family member. Each person around the table had her/his own personal candle that was kindled by passing the shamus candle from person to person. Finally the shamus candle returned to "Mama" who then kindled the last two candles, the lights of Shabbat.

Today many families in the tiny villages scattered in the remote hills and valleys of Calabria's rugged "Reventino" kindle Shabbat lights at the family table. Some place their hands on the head of each child as each personal candle is lit while bits and pieces of blessings escape from the lips of grandparents. And when asked, these families often attribute their Friday night custom to "family traditions". Others admit to having heard that "back in the day" the family may have been Jewish.

Finding and using my family's the three branch candelabra has opened my eyes and opened the door to the rich Jewish heritage that once was an integral part of Calabrian and Sicilian life. My mission, as I traverse the hills surrounding my Calabrian village, is twofold – to discover these lost traditions and to rekindle the joys of Judaism for Italian *bnei anusim* – one candle at a time.

How the Jews Named Italy

It is the determined visitor who climbs the winding mountain road (*serpentuosa*, say the locals) to the southern Italian village of Serrastretta to find Synagogue Ner Tamid del Sud, The Eternal Light of the South, the first active synagogue in Calabria in 500 years. As rabbi and founder, it is a joy and a challenge for me to work here, especially since Serrastretta is the village where all of my Italian ancestors were born and raised – an isolated town where Jews settled and practiced in secret for over four hundred years. My father, Antonio Abramo Aiello, (z"l) was raised here and often he would recall the early years spent with his crypto-Jewish family:

"When I was a boy here in the village, the public school ended with the third grade. But Mama was determined that I should continue my education. She wanted me to know Torah so she found an older gentleman to teach me. Unfortunately he lived twenty-three kilometers down the mountain. But that did not deter my mother. She found a farmer who routinely made the trip to market which meant that twice a week I sat atop artichokes, or potatoes or broccoli (How I wished for a soft 'lettuce' ride!) while the farmer drove a horse drawn cart to Timpone, the Jewish Quarter of Nicastro. He went to market and I went to study."

"I never knew my teacher's name. To me he was Maestro, and that was all. I think Jews were still afraid then of being found out. We studied Torah but his Jewish stories were the ones I liked best. Especially the one about how Italy got its name."

And then my father would tell me a story that has been a part of Calabrian Jewish lore for centuries. The story is a fascinating twist on the Chanukah legend and features the Maccabees in their life or death struggle against their Greek oppressors.

The story begins about 200 years before the Common Era. The Jews of Moadim found themselves in dire straits as King Antiochus began an assimilation program designed to separate the Jews from their culture, tradition and religious observance. We know what happened next. The Maccabees rose up in rebellion against him. But as the war dragged on and the Jews were faced with heavy losses, the Maccabees made an important decision – one that, until recently, was lost to Jewish history. In desperation these Jews decided to form scouting parties that set sail from Judea into the Mediterranean Sea in search of mercenary soldiers to help their cause. As their tiny craft drifted farther into unfamiliar waters, they saw what we recognize today as the "toe" of the Italian "boot". Then, as the Jews aboard viewed a beautiful mist rising above miles of pristine Calabrian coastline, in Hebrew they exclaimed, *"Aee-Tal-Ya"*.

What does this mean? *"A-ee"* (spelled with the letters *alef* and *yud)* is the Hebrew word for "island". *"Tal"* is the Hebrew word for *"dew"* and *"ya"* is a contracted form of one of the names of God. *"Ee-tal-ya"* or "Italia," which means "the island of God's dew".

Today there are several prominent historians whose documentation of ancient texts leads them to conclude that there is more than a grain of truth to this story – an account that these Jews, in their exuberance at finding a beautiful new land, exclaimed, *"A-ee- Tal- Ya"*, and gave Italy its name.

Whether or not we actually named this country, the Jews liked what they saw and stayed. We southern Italian Jews are the oldest Jews in the Diaspora and the only Jews in the world who settled voluntarily in a new land. Our ancestors created communities, like the ancient settlement at Bova Marina (in the deep south of the Italian peninsula) and later on we moved up through the "instep" of the "boot" as we built synagogues, schools and cemeteries, some of which are identified within *"Giudecce"* or Jewish neighborhoods that exist to this day.

So each year as we kindle our Chanukah lights, we Jews can share a slice of pizza or a plate of pasta in honor of our Italian Jewish ancestors, our *parenti* - the courageous and irrepressible Maccabees who navigated (without GPS!), and stumbled upon one of the most beautiful places on earth, *"A-ee-Tal-Ya"*, Italy, the name the ancient Jews gave to "The Island of God's Dew".

The Seder Hamishi

Italy's B'nei Anusim Revive a Secret Passover Tradition

Some historians believe that the Russian painter, Moshe Maimon's most famous work, "Marranos: Secret Seder", actually tells the story of the Seder *Hamishi*, a special Passover seder, held, not on the first or second night of Passover, but, as its name suggests, on the fifth night of the holiday. Legend has it that during the time of the Inquisition, first in Spain, then in Portugal and finally on the islands of Sicily and Sardinia and into Italy's mainland, Jews who had been forced into Christian conversion (*b'nei anusim*) were helped, surprisingly, by their Christian neighbors.

Neofiti, as these newly minted Christians were called, continued to arouse the suspicion of Inquisition authorities – so much so that gardeners, maids, cooks and nannies who worked in households of converted Jews were offered a bounty if they could catch their employer cleaning the house of *chametz* (leavened bread), changing pots, pans and dishes, or preparing *pane azimo,* or *matzah*, the unleavened bread eaten during the Passover holiday. And then, when the first night of Passover finally arrived, Inquisition soldiers, who laid in wait for the sun to set, would burst through the doors of what had once been Jewish homes, checking to see if any of these former Jews were "judaizing" - in this case, making Passover in secret.

Observing this injustice, some courageous Christians concocted a plan to help their Jewish neighbors. At great personal peril to themselves and their families (Christians who helped Jews were often tortured and murdered along with the Jews they tried to save), these Christians encouraged their Jewish neighbors to hold a seder, not on the first or second night, but, in order not to arouse the authorities' suspicions, on the fifth night. Stories are told of Christian families who allowed Jews to sneak into their Christian *cantinas,* (basement rooms) and under the cover of darkness, these Jewish neighbors first made the space kosher and then actually observed Passover complete with symbolic foods, prayers and blessings. Over the years the fifth night seder became known as the Seder *Hamishi* – a doubly appropriate name especially since *hamish* is the Yiddish word for cozy, homey and friendly.

Here in Calabria, in the deep south of Italy or what we like to call "the toe of the Italian boot", our *b'nei anusim* continue the tradition of the Seder Hamishi. Eight years ago when Sinagoga Ner Tamid del Sud ("The Eternal Light of the South") first revived the Seder Haimshi in the town of Selinunte on the island of Sicily, friends and families, both Jewish and Christian, have gathered annually to celebrate this remarkable Passover event.

Recently the Seder Hamishi 5774 was in the Calabrian town of Lamezia Terme (formerly Nicastro) near to *Timpone,* the old Jewish quarter that to this day still stands. Seder guests toured *Timpone,* lodged at the foot of the castle of King Fredrick II, a monarch who recognized the valuable contribution that these Italian Jews made to the local economy and who offered them safety and protection. Following the tour, concert violinist, Angela Amato, whose ancestors were forced into Christian conversion and who, along with her son, Ale, has returned to their Jewish roots, began this historic seder with musical selections in Ladino, the ancient Spanish-Hebrew language of the Mediterranean Jews.

Symbolic seder foods include the traditional shank bone but for us *anusim* it is coupled with the *bietola*, (blood red beet) to symbolize the lamb's blood on the doorposts that saved the firstborn in Hebrew families. Locally grown romaine lettuce (more bitter than the American variety) replaces horseradish and pieces of celery stalk, rather than parsley, serve as *karpas,* the green vegetable that is dipped in vinegar, rather than salt water. The traditional egg on the Italian seder plate is a rich brown in color, because it has been roasted for hours with onion skins, vinegar and saffron. The seder meal begins with a *primo piatto* of rice steamed with vegetables, because in our Sephardi or Mediterranean tradition, rice as well as other *kitniyot* are considered kosher for Pesach.

Roasted lamb is a must along with *mina,* a layered lasagna-type meat, spinach and *matzah* pie brought to Italy from Spain by our crypto-Jewish ancestors. Pesach *anusim* traditions begin with the lighting of the memorial candle in honor of our "forced ones", followed by the candle blessing for Shabbat and Yom Tov, sung in an ancient Ladino melody. The seder plate itself is actually a *ke'arah*, a woven basket-type tray covered with silk netting that makes a grand entrance to the seder table after the kindling of light.

At the singing of *Ha lachma anya,* the plate of *matzah* is passed shoulder to shoulder among the guests, a symbol of the heavy burden of slavery. A tin can placed at the head of the table takes center stage for the recitation of the Ten Plagues as a splash of wine punctuates each plague. When the can is filled, the younger guests carry the can into a far corner of the garden with the admonition, "*May our enemies stay far from our door*". Then it's a rousing version of *Dayenu* which features green onion stalks that guests use to tap each other, symbolizing the sound of the whips used to beat the Hebrew slaves.

For me, a *bat anusim* or "daughter of the forced ones", leading the Seder *Hamishi* each year in Southern Italy is one of the most emotional experiences of my rabbinic career. As we read the ancient blessings I recall my own family's history when my *nonna* carried candles to the cellar to kindle the lights of Shabbat. Now as each Seder *Hamishi* brings with it the realization that fear and prejudice nearly extinguished our heritage, this understanding is coupled with a deep sense of gratitude to the nameless Christians whose courage helped preserve the very traditions that I am able to enjoy today.

Each year in Calabria, we Jews, who were nearly robbed of our religion, our culture and our heritage bring the light of Pesach out of the *cantina* and into the hearts of our brothers and sisters who, after 500 years, now have a new opportunity to do as Torah commands and become "a light unto the nations". The seder concludes with the traditional wish, "Next year in Jerusalem". For me and my fellow *b'nei anusim* whom I serve here in the deep south of Italy, we add, *Baruch HaShem*, "Next year in Calabria", too.

An Italian Jewish Homecoming

The Italian Jewish Cultural Center of Calabria (IjCCC)

Visualize the map of Italy. It's shaped like a boot. Fix that image in your mind so that you can now focus first on the "foot", then the "instep" and finally the "toe". Pinpoint this area and you've found us – the *b'nei anusim* of southern Italy. We are Calabrian and Sicilian Italians who have begun to understand, accept and appreciate our ancient hidden Jewish roots.

"You can't be Jewish, you're Italian!" With my surname, "Aiello", I heard these words all my life, from Jews, from Italians, from Italian-Americans and Americans in general who held to the misconception that Italy is a wholly Catholic country and anyone with a surname ending in a vowel could not possibly be a "real" Jew. Yet Italian Jews were the first Jews in the Diaspora. We are the only Jews in the world who moved from place to place voluntarily and we are the Jews who came to the southern Italian shore from Judea during the time of the Maccabees. We are a cultural group unto ourselves. In fact there are not two but three distinctly Jewish cultural groups, Sephardim, Ashkenazim and Italian Jews (Italkim). Who knew?

For these reasons the Italian Jewish Cultural Center of Calabria (IjCCC) was born. Thanks to a generous grant by the Vuolo-Bernstein Family Foundation, I have been able to organize a study center and create cultural events that allow Calabrian and Sicilian Jews to explore their hidden past. We say in Italian, *"una gioia ed una sfida"*, "a joy and a challenge". This phrase best describes our work here in the south of Italy – work that includes uncovering a rich Jewish past complete with snippets of Jewish ritual and practice that date back to the time of the Inquisition and before.

Much has been written about the Expulsion of the Jews of Spain in 1492. At that time Jews were given two options; forced conversion in Spain or flight from the country. Those who remained, as some of my own family did, became *marranos*, an insulting term used to describe Jews who maintained the appearance of observant Christians but hung on to their own Jewish traditions through oral history and secret practice. The Spanish government just now has begun to

9

recognize the history of Spain's *marranos*. But those who chose to flee? Where did they go?

My own family's journey is not unique. From Toledo, Spain where our name was *Ayala* (formerly *El Al* in Judea), my ancestors fled to Gibraltar then to Morocco (an Aiello family member was injured in the bomb blast outside the synagogue there several years ago). From Morocco my *antenati* ran to Sicily (and some to the Aeolian island chain). But not for long. When the long arm of Torquemada's Inquisition reached further into the Kingdom of Naples, which at that time was under Spanish rule, the family moved again, this time to Calabria. Jews ran first into the "toe" of the boot and later into the mountains and hills of "the instep".

My own family members with names like Aiello, Scalise, Mascaro, Nicotera, Grande and Marucca searched for religious freedom. When they did not find it, many of them submitted to forced conversion and maintained their Jewish traditions in the *cantina,* the basement of their homes where they lit Shabbat candles, prayed in Hebrew and studied the Five Books of Moses (the Torah). Professor Vincenzo Villella whose slim volume, *La Judeca di Nicastro*, (The Jewish Quarter of Nicastro) recounts the history of the Jews of Calabria contends that at one time we Jews numbered more than 40 percent of the entire population of Sicily and Calabria.

Armed with these statistics and with a strong emotional connection to my own roots, I bought a house in my father's hometown of Serrastretta and began to uncover my own history as well as the history of all of these Jews who once lived, worked and prospered literally in my backyard.

The work of the IjCCC includes collecting personal stories from friends and family members. We offer to any and all who are interested, the chance to learn more about the Jewish traditions of our area. To this end we organized three important events to open the door of Jewish understanding to those who believe that they have Jewish ancestry. These events were the culmination of the consistent presence of the IjCCC within the Calabrian community – a presence characterized by an open door, a welcoming hand and an open heart. As Jews, we do not proselytize. Instead, we offer the hand of Jewish welcome to those who sometimes tiptoe through the door of new learning and understanding. These efforts resulted in several significant community activities:

The Shabbaton – a weekend long experience of Jewish thought, ritual and belief. We held our first Shabbaton in 2007, an event that began with a Kabbalat Shabbat teaching service. Dozens of Calabrians from near and far attended the event that began in Lamezia Terme and continued in the synagogue in Serrastretta. Participants were introduced to Shabbat observance as I explained the ritual and meaning of lighting Shabbat candles, the blessing the children and making Kiddush.

The Shabbaton continued on Saturday morning, which began with participants boarding a "Pullman", a sturdy passenger bus for the trip up the mountain to the new synagogue, Ner Tamid del Sud (The Eternal Light of the South). Here we offered a morning Torah service and a Holy Books study, a demonstration of kosher cooking (and eating!), and a teaching experience for making Chanukah at home. We concluded with Havdalah, the service to conclude Shabbat, complete with Jewish music and dancing.

Sunday morning offered a three-hour intensive Hebrew language course as well as individual meetings to share our personal stories of hidden Jewish heritage.

We were astounded by what our participants told us:

Carolina: *"My parents always lit one candle on Friday night and made a special meal. We never knew why."* (An ancient Shabbat tradition also common to the *marranos* of Spain)

Adelina: *"When my grandfather died we covered all the mirrors in white and sat on small low chairs. We ate eggs after the funeral. My nonno asked that he not be buried by a priest or have a rosary put in his hand. Instead he asked that we stay at home for seven days and remember him."* (Jewish mourning customs, including sitting Shiva)

Raffaele: *"We stayed inside all day on Good Friday. My parents told me it was dangerous to be out. We didn't know why."* (In some parts of Italy Jews were taunted or beaten on Good Friday)

Angela: *"When we cooked with eggs, we broke each one separately to see if there was a blood spot. If so, we did not use the egg."* (kosher tradition)

Ennio: *"When there was a wedding the bride and groom received a coperta, a special lace cover. It was held over their heads while the fathers made a blessing and then given to the couple as the covering for the marriage bed."* (the "chuppah" or wedding canopy)

Our introductory event was so successful that the IjCCC organized a Chanukah Open House for all those with Jewish stories to share. The event was open to the public, especially to those who had a family interest in learning about this wintertime festival. A group of 45 Calabrians, ranging in age from 14 to 88 came to the event with a desire to learn more. To our surprise and honor our local parish priest, Don Gigi Iuliano, also attended as well as Sindaco Renato Mascaro, the mayor of our town.

Once again, special time was set aside to share family memories that indicated possible Jewish ancestry. Don Gigi was especially moved. He read from the Book of Maccabees and led the group in singing *Hevinu Shalom Alechem*, amazingly the Jewish hymn that is sung in churches in our local mountain-top *anusim* communities!

The priest also spoke of his own Jewish heritage and encouraged the group to explore theirs. Rabbi and priest together recalled the words of the late Pope John Paul II who noted that the Jews are the older brothers and sisters of the Christians and as such openly encouraged interfaith dialogue.

As our first Shabbaton drew to a close the IjCCC pledged to continue its sacred mission and indeed we have! We offer Shabbaton weekends twice each year where conversion students and interested *anusim* join us in Calabria to learn about and experience hands-on Jewish traditions. Each Shabbaton is infused with our basic purpose and our deep commitment – to extend the hand of Jewish welcome to southern Italians who have waited so long and so patiently to finally come home.

For more information about the IjCCC and Synagogue Ner Tamid del Sud see www.rabbibarbara.com

Italy's Five Books of Miriam

Five Young Women Reclaim Torah As Their Own

Given the scope of Jewish history with all of its ancient traditions, it wasn't all that long ago that Judaism celebrated the first girl in modern times to become a Bat Mitzvah. It happened in America in 1922 when Rabbi Mordechai Kaplan, the founder of the Reconstructionist movement, arranged for his daughter, Judith to become a Bat Mitzvah in a public synagogue ceremony.

Today we make the assumption that the Bat Mitzvah moment occurs when the young girl reads from the Torah scroll – an entirely logical belief especially since these days the girls assist the rabbi on the *bima*, lead prayers and blessings and read Torah, just as the boys have always done. But for Judith Kaplan, our first American Bat Mitzvah, that wasn't the case. Instead history records that young Judith did not receive a full *aliyah* which means that she did not make the blessings before and after the Torah reading or read directly from the scroll itself. And although her experience represented a monumental change in what had been described as patriarchal Judaism, Judith's Bat Mitzvah ceremony is described as "a much diminished version of what the boys did".

In fact we now understand that the first American Bat Mitzvah resembled what Jewish girls in Italy had done for centuries. Back in the 1600's Italian girls stood before the open ark, recited a special prayer, received the rabbi's blessing and then adjourned for the *Sedudat Mitzvah*, the celebratory meal held in the girl's home. Some suggest that Rabbi Kaplan actually may have studied this ancient Italian ceremony and adapted it for his daughter's rite.

So, who knew? The Bat Mitzvah ceremony has its roots in early 17th century Italy, a fact that, as Jewish rituals evolve and change, connects the five young women who became the very first in Italy to advance the ancient Bat Mitzvah tradition and read directly from the Sefer Torah.

Because Miriam is the very first individual in the Torah to be called a prophet, it occurred to me that it would be entirely natural to celebrate this feminist achievement by referring to my first five B'not Mitzvah as Italy's "Five Books of Miriam".

When I read Dr. Ellen Frankel's wonderful book (The Five Books of Miriam, Putnam, 1966) which represents the first Torah commentary from a woman's point of view, I was encouraged. I found that Frankel's book has done much to advance the conversation regarding Jewish women and their Jewish traditions and these five young girls are Italy's contribution to this important process.

It all began with *Dina bat Miriam v' Julio*, Camila S. At the time Camila lived in Rome with her parents and two sisters and recalls the happy celebration when her older sister became Bat Mitzvah in Los Angeles, California. Camila had a vivid memory of her sister standing on the *bima*, reading from the Torah scroll. Camila was enchanted and she looked forward to having the same experience. When her parents took her to Tempio Maggiore (The Great Synaogue of Rome), an orthodox synagogue as are all the synagogues throughout Italy, Camila witnessed something entirely different from what she was expecting.

Camila recalls that the girl came up to the *bima,* but was not permitted to read from the scroll. Instead an older brother read from the Torah in her honor. Camila's mother recalls her daughter's exact words that morning. "I'm not doing that!" – a statement that initiated the family's journey to create the egalitarian ceremony that, to mother and daughter, only seemed right.

In July 2005 at a ceremony attended by friends and family from New York, Los Angeles, Brazil, Poland and Israel, Camila became the first young woman in Italian history to be called to the Torah, to touch the Torah and to read directly from the Torah scroll.

In June 2010, Charis F-M. traveled with her family to Calabria, to Synagogue Ner Tamid del Sud, the first active synagogue in Calabria in 500 years since Inquisition times. There as *Tzipa bat Chana v'Zalman*, Charis became Italy's second Bat Mitzvah in the modern tradition and the first girl in Calabria's history to follow in Camila's footsteps and read directly from the Torah scroll.

Leila S., Camila's younger sister, became Bat Mitzvah number three. Again in Rome and following her older sister's lead, Leila studied with Rabbi Barbara long distance via Skype internet video telephone. In May 2010 Leila carried the Torah in procession (*hakafah*) through a crowd of more than one hundred friends and family and then opened the sacred scroll to read verses from *Parasha Naso.*

June 2011 marked a Bat Mitzvah first for Tuscany when Louisa A. became the fourth girl in all of Italy and the first girl in Tuscany to become a Torah-reading Bat Mitzvah. Known in Hebrew as *Aliza bat Ariel v' Yehuda*, Louisa shares her Hebrew name with author Aliza Lavie whose landmark siddur, A Jewish Woman's Prayer Book, has been translated into Italian and is used today throughout Italy. The book details the trials, challenges and joys of Jewish women throughout the centuries and the text reflects an alternative model, based in the feminine experience.

With Samantha G.'s ceremony held in the Calabria synagogue, Rabbi Barbara's "Five Books of Miriam" are complete. Samantha, whose Hebrew name is *Savanah bat Chaya v' Dan,* her parents, brothers and grandparents traveled from Florida to the deep south of Italy to experience Shabbat, Italian style. Making *kiddush* under the ancient grape arbor, complete with local wine and handmade *challah*, offered Samantha and her family an opportunity to experience Judaism in an isolated mountain community founded centuries ago by Italian crypto-Jews escaping persecution.

In The Women's Torah Commentary, Rabbi Sue Levi Ewell writes, "Contemporary Jews have begun to reclaim Miriam as a model for biblical leadership. As (we) break Miriam's silence and restore her memory as prophet and teacher, all of our songs are enriched and our people's story becomes more whole."

As a woman rabbi in the modern tradition, I like to think that in memory and in honor of Prophet Miriam, our young women, Camila, Charis, Leila, Louisa and Samantha have accelerated the acceptance and the equality of women throughout Italy and beyond.

The Cat That Ate the Cannoli

During the warm summer months our little synagogue in Bella Italia springs to life. Both my home and the synagogue I founded in 2006 are located in the tiny village of Serrastretta, in Calabria mountains, near the "toe" of the Italian "boot," and throughout the late spring and early summer we welcome Bar and Bat Mitzvah families from around the world who want to give their children an understanding that there are places on the planet where it's not easy to be Jewish.

A visit to our synagogue, Ner Tamid del Sud, (The Eternal Light of the South) makes the point. As the first and only active synagogue in the south of Italy since Inquisition times, we offer a pluralistic approach to Judaism in that we are open and welcoming to Jews of all backgrounds. We extend the hand of Jewish welcome to interfaith families, gay and lesbian couples and their children and *b'nei anusim*, Italians whose Jewish roots go back centuries to the time when they were forced into Christian conversion.

During a recent summer we had the honor and delight to welcome eight Bar and Bat Mitzvah families from Italy and the United States. All of us, including many of our local members, *kvelled* as children from California, Chicago, Washington, DC, Rome, Naples and Jamaica read from our antique Torah scroll that dates back to 1783.

In Italy we have a saying, *"i quattro gatti"* – "The Four Cats," which is used to describe a very under-attended event. For example someone might ask, "So how was the turn-out for the lecture?" If there were fewer participants than expected, the response might be, *"Ci sono stati quattro gatti."* – "There were four cats!" which means that attendance was not so good.

In 2006 when we dedicated our Calabrian synagogue, we were the synagogue *"di quattro gatti,"* the synagogue of "the four cats," in more ways than one. In the early days we worked hard to help local Italians discover and embrace their Jewish roots and slowly, very slowly, residents of our village and surrounding towns began to demonstrate that they wanted to learn more about their ancient

17

Jewish heritage. Some Shabbat mornings we hosted five or six congregants and there were services where it was difficult to make a minyan. Synagogue Ner Tamid del Sud began as the synagogue of "the four cats!"

And then there is the fact that, yes. indeed, we really do have four cats! There's Toppi, Tullio, Tommasina and Tobia, all of whom welcome our local and international guests to the shul. Our Bar and Bat Mitzvah boys and girls are delighted with our friendly critters and when Domenico, the local photographer arrives to shoot the family photos, most of them want at least one picture with the cats.

So that's how it was when Maddy and her family from California came to Serrastretta for her Bat Mitzvah ceremony. All was going well until just before the Torah service, when Maddy burst into giggles. We all looked in Maddy's direction to see what tickled her so and then we saw him. There was black cat, Toppi, perched on the *oneg* table, holding one of our cannoli in his mouth, wiggling it, Grouch Marx style, like he was smoking a cigar!

Later on as we made *kiddush* under the grape arbor, Maddy mused that becoming Bat Mitzvah in Italy was truly a unique experience. She was touched that she stood on a mountain top in a tiny synagogue with Italians who want so much to be Jewish that some of them had traveled hundreds of kilometers just to share the service with her. "And not only that," Maddy said. "I'll bet I'm the only girl who shared her Bat Mitzvah with the cat that ate the cannoli!"

Walter Finds His Way

A Ben Anusim Becomes Calabria's First Adult Bar Mitzvah

It was nearly ten years ago when Walter Aiello began his own Jewish journey. Back then he was interested in determining if his Aiello surname had ancient Jewish origins and if any of his family's traditions, which were often dismissed as strange and unusual, had any definite Jewish connection.

"I'm a Brooklyn boy", Walter says with noticeable pride in his voice and he goes on to explain how his artisan father made it in America by crafting life-like, artistic mannequin hands. But it was Santos Aiello, Walter's grandfather, who posthumously offered the first clue. Walter heard his father, Luigi say that grandfather was proud of his name and that the pronunciation of the Aiello surname was *"A-ee-yo"*. Grandpa's assertion that the family surname should always be given the correct Spanish pronunciation was an audible reminder of what Walter would discover to be his family's Jewish roots dating back to the Expulsion of the Jews from Spain.

Based on what he had heard as a child, Walter initiated a search with the Italian Jewish Cultural Center of Calabria (IjCCC), our research and archival group dedicated to the discovery of the Jewish heritage behind the surnames found today in Calabria and Sicily. Using documents which describe the persecution, arrest and murder of Jewish families and combing through ancient lists of Jewish family surnames, historian Vincenzo Villella and archivist Enrico Mascaro determined that Walter's case was one of many that connected a deeply felt attraction with a lost Jewish identity.

But Walter didn't stop there. Over the years he became involved with the Jewish community, taking part in the organization of a program to help persons with disabilities participate more fully in synagogue life. Later on when Walter's beloved wife became seriously ill, Walter took his first tentative steps to becoming fully Jewish. Jewish friends offered to stay with Walter's wife so that he could go to Shabbat synagogue services- an important weekly event that offered him spiritual solace and a consistent Jewish experience. With the support of a loving and caring rabbi, (Rabbi Leah Berkowitz), Walter became a

Jew By Choice in 2012 at the Judea Reform Synagogue in Raleigh, North Carolina.

One year later Walter's Jewish Journey came full circle when he traveled to Italy to the tiny Calabrian village of Serrastsretta to become a Bar Mitzvah at Sinagoga Ner Tamid del Sud, the first active synagogue in Calabria since Inquisition times. Tall and lean and with an American accent, at first sight one might assume that although his *"cognome"* Aiello, is one of Italy's oldest Jewish surnames, Walter might not feel comfortable in this isolated mountain town. But that was not the case. "I feel like I've come home", Walter said as he entered the tiny sanctuary, accompanied by his two adult sons. And indeed he had as Walter's eyes filled with tears as he began to read from the ancient Torah scroll.

Local *"Serrastrettese"*, many of whom also have lost and hidden Jewish roots, applauded Walter's accomplishment, especially the fact that at 69 years of age, he had completed his Jewish journey and returned to claim his heritage.

Walter is back in North Carolina now but recently he took the time to share his thoughts about his experience with us here in Calabria. Walter writes, "(I am) recalling how my arrival at Serrastretta was like returning to a forgotten childhood home after a long absence."

On May 16, 2013 Walter Aiello became our synagogue's first adult Bar Mitzvah as he read from the Torah scroll in our newly expanded sanctuary. As Walter's Italian rabbi, and most likely a part of his extended *"mispachah"* (Yes, I believe we are related!), I couldn't be more pleased, proud and honored not only to officiate at Walter's Bar Mitzvah celebration, but even more to continue our mission to welcome yet another of the B'nei Anusim *"a casa ancora."* Home again.

NOTE: For more information on discovering Italian Jewish roots or becoming Bar or Bat Mitzvah in Calabria see www.rabbibarbara.com

The Midnight Shofar

The Hills of Calabria Reveal an Ancient Jewish Tradition

It is New Year's Eve in Calabria, the deep south of the Italian peninsula. At the stroke of midnight the bells in the church tower in the tiny village of Serrastretta ring twelve times. But if you are very quiet and the night is very still, you will hear something more. From deep in the forest of the Reventino, a local Calabrian mountain range located in the "instep" of the "boot", you will hear first one, then another, then another long low moan of the ancient ram's horn.

The same ram's horn that in Hebrew is called the *shofar!* The same ram's horn that inaugurates *Rosh HaShanah*, the Jewish New Year. Yet for centuries on the night that marks the beginning of the secular New Year, families in southern Italy blow a shofar-like instrument that is the hallmark of the Jewish celebration that occurs, not in December, but in the autumn of the year.

It is a custom that on the surface seems strange, but a deeper look into the life and traditions of the *b'nei anusim* (a Hebrew term that means "the forced ones") who inhabit this area makes sense of it all. Centuries ago, during Inquisition times, the Jews of Spain and Portugal had one of two choices; convert to Christianity or leave their homes. Those Jews who were forced from Spain and Portugal found refuge on the island of Sicily and on the tiny islands that make up the Aeolian chain. There they lived in relative peace until the long arm of the Inquisition reached them there as well. Forced to flee yet again, Jewish families made their way onto the Italian mainland, first to the "toe" and then north through the "foot" of the Italian "boot" and into the Calabrian mountains.

For centuries these Jewish families lived in relative safety but fear is a *minestra*, a soup that cooks slowly. Stories of persecution, arrests and public burnings percolate through these mountains – so much so that if one were to ask about a family's Jewish heritage, the downcast eyes and blank expressions say it all. That's why it is such a great challenge to connect these Italian *b'nei anusim* with their Jewish history. But for me, the first rabbi of the first synagogue in Calabria since Inquisition times, it is a *"sfida e gioia"* a challenge and a joy.

During my nearly twelve years in the Calabrian hills I've finally learned to ask the right questions. No longer do I ask, "Do you think your family was once Jewish?" No. Calabrians have learned that admitting to a Jewish heritage can be dangerous. Instead I ask, "What does your family do when a baby is born? When a couple marries? What is a funeral like for your family? How do you mourn? Do you have special family customs to celebrate the holidays?" That is how I learned about the shofar at midnight.

Francesco, a local baker, explained it all to me when he said, "*Tanti anni fa… Many years ago our families celebrated a different new year. It was the at the harvest time when we found a ram and made his horn into a musical instrument. But it was dangerous to be different so we learned to wait. To wait for the last day of the year when everyone else was celebrating. Now there are fireworks and trumpet blasts. When the ram's horn is sounded, it is not so strange anymore.*"

Cautiously I asked Francesco, "Do you know that the ram's horn is a Jewish tradition?" Francesco replies that he once heard something like that but he prefers to say that the practice is an ancient family tradition.

And so it goes. For centuries we Calabrians took our Jewish traditions into our homes and our hearts and slowly, at first for safety reasons, and then for cultural reasons, the religious meanings of these rituals were lost. Our precious Jewish customs became family traditions and sadly, nothing more. It has become my mission and my passion to uncover more of these family traditions that were once a part of a thriving Jewish past. It is my hope that I can continue to give my Calabrian relatives, my *meshpucha*, the *b'nei anusim* who have so carefully and cautiously preserved the vestiges of their Jewish heritage, an opportunity to discover and embrace their Jewish roots.

Becca's Wooden Box

A Jewish Father's Legacy for His Sicilian Daughter

She arrived on Sunday morning, having received an announcement of our meeting several days before. At first she was not certain that the gathering would be appropriate for her, but curiosity overcame her fear and she found herself at the door of an apartment in Palermo, Sicily ready to begin what she hoped would be a positive Jewish journey.

Becca (not her real name) brought her enthusiasm and questions to Chavurah Ner Tamid Palermo. *Chavurah* is a Hebrew word that means *group of friends*, and *Ner Tamid* is the Hebrew phrase for "eternal light". Founded in 2005, this group of friends comprises a small but determined modern Jewish congregation, dedicated to helping people like Becca establish and embrace their Jewish heritage. Ner Tamid Palermo represents a tiny but strong Jewish flame that, although the persecutions of the Inquisition tried to extinguish it, the light of Judaism never died. Dedicated to *the b'nei anusim* of Sicily – those who were forced into Christian conversion nearly 500 years ago, Ner Tamid Palermo offers a unique opportunity for men and women like Becca to share their stories and make a personal Jewish connection.

We gathered around the table and began our meeting with a discussion of modern pluralistic Jewish traditions and concluded with *Havdalah*, the Saturday evening service that marks the end of the Jewish Sabbath (*Shabbat*). But it was on Sunday morning, at our Torah study when Becca arrived with a remarkable story to tell.

"I always knew we were Jewish," she began, but then added, "I should say I always knew we were different. Later I came to believe that our difference was that we were not Christian but Jewish." Becca's expression, animated now, told the story of her third grade classmates and how they prepared for their First Communion. "My father, who has since passed away, would not permit me to make the First Communion. I was a little girl and I was very confused. And then there was the wooden box."

As Becca's story unfolded, our little group fell silent. Some of us were on the edge of our chairs as we listened to Becca describe the locked wooden box that

23

her father said held their family's treasures. Over the years Becca asked her father to open the box and share these wonderful items that she was certain were locked inside. But Papa' never would. After he died, Becca found the box and assumed that the treasures were personal mementos. Love letters, perhaps and nothing more.

The day came, however when Becca's sadness subsided and her curiosity about the box returned. With screwdriver in hand, she broke the lock on the wooden box. Slowly she opened it to find "This!" she exclaimed, extending her hand for us to see. It was a bracelet and etched on it in silver was a delicate *"Magen David"*, Star of David.

Becca went on to explain that the box also contained a silver pointer that she later leaned was called by the Hebrew word, *yad.* A *yad* is used during the synagogue service. It is held by the Torah reader, who, as she/he reads each word of the scroll, touches each word as it is read. Finally a Hebrew book, an ancient *siddur* (prayer book), also saw the light of day in Becca's hands.

While we sat in silence, absorbed in Becca's family story, Vincenzo, our *"colla"*, the "glue" of our Chavurah noted, "This is the reason we are here today. We are here to give voice to our hidden Jewish experiences, to unlock them as Becca has unlocked her father's box."

The Pluralistic Jewish movement, of which Ner Tamid Palermo is a part, is a modern approach to Judaism, that observes *halakah* (Jewish law) as it was intended by our rabbinic sages. Because the word *halakah* derives from the Hebrew word, *holech* which means "to walk", Pluralistic Judaism moves forward, advances and adapts, just as the ancient concept implies.

Ner Tamid Palermo, along with its parent congregation in Calabria, Ner Tamid del Sud, extends the hand of Jewish welcome to Jews of all backgrounds, most especially to the *"b'nei anusim"* of southern Italy who so desperately want to claim their Jewish traditions that were stolen from them centuries ago.

"Who knows," said Vincenzo. "All throughout Sicily there may be hundreds of stories locked in wooden boxes." Ner Tamid Palermo continues its commitment to symbolically find those boxes, unlock the family stories, and extend the hand of friendship and love to our *anusim* brothers and sisters as we say to them, "Welcome Home."

Vincenzo's Victory

An Anusim Bar Mitzvah in Palermo, Sicily

The surnames of Vincenzo's ancestors appear on ancient Inquisition documents that describe the arrest, torture and murder of Sicilian Jews. Many of these were families who were forced to accept Christian baptism but refused to abandon their Jewish practices. When these secret Jews were found to be "Judaizing," they were thrown into jail, tortured and often burned alive in public spectacles called *autodafe*`.

Reclaiming their Judaism has been difficult for many secret Jews, called *bnei anusim*, or "children of the forced ones," so it was with great joy and pride that Vincenzo Uziel Li Calzi, a Sicilian *ben anusim* made Jewish history by becoming the third person to have a public Bar Mitzvah ceremony on the island of Sicily in 500 years since Inquisition times.

"Sono molto commosso," (That's Italian for "I'm so *verklempt!*"), said Vincenzo as he made his way to the reading table where an antique Torah scroll (inscribed in 1783) was open and ready for his historic reading. As tears streamed down his cheeks, Vincenzo's overwhelming emotion at being called to the Torah touched us all, in large part because for decades Vincenzo, who is now nearly 70 years old, tried his best to convince Italy's Jewish bureaucracy that his family's ancient Jewish practices qualified him as a Jew. But the Christian conversions that were forced upon Sicilian Jews often meant that Jewish traditions were hidden. Most Jewish rituals were practiced in secret, so for Jews like Vincenzo, no formal documentation exists that confirms a family's Jewish heritage. The result was that many *b'nei anusim* aroused suspicion among Italy's established Jewish organizations and like Vincenzo, most were never welcomed into traditional Jewish communities.

It wasn't until 2004, the year that modern Pluralistic Judaism came to Sicily, when Vincenzo and other *b'nei anusim* were given the recognition they deserved. And when Vincenzo learned that Pluralistic Judaism was an option for *anusim*, he did all he could to make this vital Jewish connection. "I wanted to be recognized as a Jew, Vincenzo says, "so I phoned up Rabbina Barbara." It was that phone call that led me to my relationship with this very special man.

The first step was a meeting between me and my potential student, which meant a trip from Milan to Palermo to find out more about Vincenzo's Jewish heritage and how, as a rabbi and a *bat anusim* myself, I could help him connect with the faith of his ancestors. What I found amazed me. Although his physical strength had been compromised to the extent that he needed crutches to walk and help to steady his shaking hands, Vincenzo's spiritual energy was remarkable. Self - taught in the basic Shabbat blessings, this slight elderly gentleman, challenged by disabilities that would overwhelm most of us, was a tower of strength when it came to the study and practice of Judaism.

Immediately I suggested that Vincenzo join our distance learning program designed especially for *b'nei anusim* who live in remote towns and tiny villages throughout Sicily, Calabria and the Aeolian Islands. Following a year's study, Vincenzo was ready for his *Bet Din* and yet another challenge. Because his health concerns prohibited travel, how could Vincenzo meet with the three rabbis who had come to Milan to examine our students? When I suggested a telephone meeting, the rabbis enthusiastically agreed and that's how it happened that Vincenzo Li Calzi, *ben anusim*, sat before his telephone in Palermo and, dressed formally in a suit and tie, answered the questions posed to him by the London rabbis. Shortly afterward, at a Sicilian beach under a radiant Italian sky, I organized Vincenzo's *mikveh*, the traditional ritual immersion, and presented him with his certificate as a proud MOT, or Member of the Tribe!

Vincenzo's Jewish journey was just beginning as he and others in Palermo formed the first active congregation in Sicily since the evils of the Inquisition's forced conversions nearly wiped out Sicily's Jewish population. Our new congregation, Ner Tamid Palermo (the Eternal Light of Palermo) represented the flame that could not be extinguished, thanks to the efforts of "new Jews" like Vincenzo.

In the intervening years, Vincenzo and others organized Chanukah celebrations and Passover seders, and Vincenzo and his wife Amalia continue to open their home to men and women throughout Sicily who come to tell the stories of their hidden Jewish heritage and how they hope to reclaim their Jewish identity.

"You can't miss your Bar Mitzvah," Vincenzo said one day during our weekly telephone meetings. As leader of Palermo's *chavurah*, Vincenzo added, "I know that when he reaches thirteen years, the boy is a Bar Mitzvah, but one can have the ceremony at any age, so, *Rabbina,* now it is time for my Bar Mitzvah ceremony."

After six months of study, again via the telephone, during which time Vincenzo learned not only how to read his Torah verses but to chant them in ancient Italian trope, he was ready. Thanks to the generosity of the Palermo Valdesian Church (a Christian denomination whose Italian history also includes suffering and persecution), Congregation Ner Tamid Palermo was able to create sacred Jewish space in the church's meeting room in order to celebrate this historic Jewish event.

On Shabbat morning, May 17, 2014, Vincenzo realized his dream. Family and friends gathered for the *Shacharit* service and enjoyed Vincenzo's beautiful chanting of the prayers and blessings including the Shabbat *Kedusha.* For the *hakafah*, or Torah procession, I carried the Torah in Vincenzo's honor as his wife took his arm and guided him through the congregation. When it was time to read from the scroll, the entire room burst into the chant that calls a Jew to the Torah; "*Ya'amod a Sefer Torah, Uziel ben Avraham v' Sarah, HaBar Mitzvah!*" Leaning on his crutches, Vincenzo stood, *yad* in hand, and read from the ancient Hebrew scroll. Then, to the shouts of *HaZaak* and *Mazel Tov*, the enthusiastic crowd tossed wrapped candies in Vincenzo's direction, symbolically showering him with blessing upon blessing.

At the *oneg* that followed, a number of guests wanted to know more about the modern pluralistic movement that extends the hand of Jewish welcome to Jews of all backgrounds, including *b'nei anusim*. "Is it true," a young woman asked, "that Ner Tamid Palermo is open to everyone including interfaith families, traditional Jews, and gay and lesbian couples and their children?" Another asked, "Can women read from the Torah and participate equally with men?" A smiling Vincenzo was happy to affirm that as part of the Pluralistic Jewish movement, "We do not separate men and women and we are open to all."

"Creating a pluralistic Jewish congregation has been a challenge," Vincenzo said, referring to the advent of a large Israeli based organization, orthodox in practice that recently arrived in the city, purporting to have "discovered" the secret Jews of Palermo – a situation that has created divisiveness and confusion. "Goliaths may come," said Vincenzo, "but we Pluralistic Jews are the little Davids and our faith makes us strong."

For Vincenzo, his Bar Mitzvah celebration was a personal victory, not only for him but for all of Sicily's *b'nei anusim* who, after 500 years, want so much to be recognized as the Jews they once were. Vincenzo's Bar Mitzvah ceremony is a milestone, for not only was a life-long dream realized, but for Sicilian Jews who were able to celebrate their ten year anniversary of pluralism, perseverance and faith, Vincenzo's victory is a victory for all of us.

Saro's Search

"My Father's Dying Words"

It was springtime several years ago as the Jewish world celebrated Pesach, that Saro A. uncovered something quite troubling. Saro's roots are anusim, (see * definition below) something he discovered some 25 years ago when his father's dying words were *Elohim, Elohim*. After several years of dogged research, Saro discovered the secret behind the whispered *Elohim*. Saro was astounded to learn that *Elohim* is a Hebrew word for one of the names of God. With only *Elohim* to guide him, Saro began a quest to find out who he really was.

Later on, following his two years of study and subsequent conversion to the Jewish religion, Saro began his own study of his family's roots. He learned that his ancestors were a part of the lost Jews of Sicily, and they were directly connected to a town with a horrifying history. During the Christian celebration of Holy Week, which includes ritual observance of the day of Jesus' death, a *spettacolo*, or "show" was held in a small village near the town of Messina.

There on "Good Friday", bands of townspeople dressed themselves in the bright red vests and gaudy yellow hats that once served as cruel reminders of how Jews were forced to identify themselves and how Jews were separated from the general population. Others wore masks that depicted the Jews as the devil. These "characters" marched through the streets of the small village of San Fratello while other townspeople chased and beat "the Jews". News reports indicated that for the last several years the "celebration" has become violent. Fueled by alcohol, roving bands of drunken citizens raced through town, hell-bent on doing real damage to the real Jews who lived nearby. This "celebration" is a part of Saro A.'s Jewish roots.

Today in Italy a debate rages about whether festivals like the one enacted each year in Sicily are cultural in nature or are merely examples of profound discrimination and intolerance. In some Italian villages, the crucifix still hangs in every public school classroom and every government office. Citizens ask themselves, is the cross an example of Italian culture or does it symbolize state sponsored religious exclusivity?

In a country where Catholicism is entrenched in almost every aspect of life, where do Jews fit in? And what about the Jews of the deep south of Italy - the Jews whose roots are deep in the "foot" of the boot? What can be done to help Italian *anusim* who once numbered nearly 50 percent of the entire Italian population of southern Italy but who now identify themselves as forced converts who practiced as secret Jews?

As an Italian Jew whose family originates in Calabria, I have firsthand experience with the loss of Jewish heritage and tradition. My grandmother, Felicia Scalise, observed in secret, carrying her Shabbat candles underground into the cantina where she kindled the lights of Shabbat far away from the eyes of neighbors and even from other *converso* relatives as well. My father, Antonio Aiello, (z"l) who knew only bits and pieces of prayers and celebrations, observed Havdalah (the concluding service of Shabbat) in the only way he knew how - by pointing to three stars and chanting "*Baruch, Baruch, Baruch!*"

Over the years I have met many other Italians like myself who are eager to affirm their Jewishness and learn more about family traditions that were stolen from them 500 years ago. Becoming a rabbi was a turning point in my life for many reasons. Not only do I have the opportunity and the joy to serve my people, but now that I live and work in Italy, in the heart of the Calabrian mountains, I have returned to my roots. Finally I have the joy and the challenge to serve Italians like myself who are hungry to know who they really are.

In January 2004, the mayor of Lamezia Terme (the largest town near to my ancestral village) dedicated a plaque to acknowledge a Jewish presence in our area that dates back to the 1200's. In front of the archway that leads to the old Jewish Quarter, called *Timpone*, ("the ridge") we find words that complement the Jews who once lived there on their "industrious and vibrant community". And indeed it was.

The making of silk, the development of indigo dye and the design and production of leather goods were activities originated by the Jews of Nicastro (as Lamezia Terme was once called). These Jews brought their skills to Calabria from Spain, after the Expulsion of Spanish Jews in the late 1490's. Indeed a remnant of the original *Timpone* synagogue exists, (currently a Catholic Church has been built over it) and I have been able to find the original *mikveh*, in a garden near the synagogue site.

In his book, *La Judeca di Nicastro e la storia degli Ebrei in Calabria*, (The Jewish Quarter of Nicastro and the history of the Jews of Calabria) author Vincenzo Villella describes the rich cultural and religious life of the Jews of Southern Italy.

From the discriminatory practices that included the requirement that men wear a yellow hat to designate their Jewishness and Jewish women wear the blue veil of the prostitute, Professor Villella offers a description of our Italian ancestors who were courageous and tenacious in the face of prejudice and persecution.

In 2015 author Villella revised and expanded his book, now titled *Giudecce de Calabria*, (The Jewish Quarters of Calabria) to include descriptions of the dozens of tiny villages that once featured a vibrant Jewish presence, along with a comprehensive list of Italian surnames that are Jewish in origin. This list has been an invaluable tool for Calabrians to uncover their Jewish history and reclaim their rightful place among Jews worldwide.

Over ten years ago, when I first arrived in Calabria I had the opportunity to discuss Professor Villella's work in the context of my own *anusim* background. A local Catholic priest offered the church social hall as a venue where I could tell my story. Following my presentation, parish priest, Don Natale Colafati encouraged those who felt they had Jewish roots to join me for a private meeting.

Amazingly, a large group of Calabrians pushed forward for the private meeting. Many described themselves as "secular" because they had never felt comfortable with Catholic tradition, while others shared stories of a Jewish past that for decades had only been whispered about behind closed doors. Some of the attendees were acutely aware of the forced conversions that date back to the time when the Inquisition reached into southern Italy and some related how, as children, they were taught that participating in Catholic ritual was "to act in a play", because God knew that they were *"ebrei del cuore"*, "Jews of the heart".

The emotion of that initial meeting has never left me. In fact it has been the driving force behind the organization of our cultural center (IjCCC) and synagogue (Ner Tamid del Sud) both of which are devoted to extending the hand of Jewish welcome to Italians in Italy, and to Italians around the world who, despite the fact that their precious Jewish traditions were driven underground, these courageous and determined *anusim* maintained a light in the soul that never died.

Halachic definition of "anusim." "Anusim," plural for anús, means forced ones in Hebrew. This is rabbinic legal terminology applied to a Jew who has been forced to abandon Judaism against his or her will, and who does whatever is in his or her power to continue practicing Judaism under the forced condition. It derives from the Talmudic term abera be'ones [Abodá Zará 54a]. (From Wikipedia)

Emma's Dilemma

"The Real Jews Are the Dead Ones"

Emma D. (not her real name) is a *bat anusim* – a Hebrew term which translates as "the daughter of the forced ones". Her Italian Jewish roots, tangled as they are, also run deep. Emma traces her ancestry back 500 years to Inquisition times when Jews were forced to either convert to Christianity or face jail, expulsion or death.

Unlike Emma's ancestors, there were Jews of means in Spain and later in Sicily and in Calabria (the "toe" of the Italian "boot") who were able to sell their possessions or hand over their gold in order to book passage that would take them to safety. Other Jews were not so fortunate. Unable to escape, they submitted to Christian conversion while hiding their Jewish traditions within their immediate families.

In fact, Inquisition records document Jewish families with surnames the same as Emma's, who were denounced to Church authorities for "Judaizing" by their very own cooks, housemaids and gardeners. Many of these families were arrested and burned alive in the public square. Those who survived often became practicing Catholics and only on rare occasions would they trust the precious secret of their Jewish ancestry to other members of their extended families.

Deathbed confessions were not unusual. One *bat anusim* from a Calabrian mountain village known historically as having been an ancient Jewish settlement recounts her grandmother's final hours. As *Nonna* hovered near death she asked for her children and as they gathered she said, "When I die, do not call the priest. Do not place a rosary in my hands. Wrap my body in a white sheet and bury me the next day." As the curious family looked on, *Nonna* concluded, "I never told you. We are Jews."

Although Emma's family has no deathbed drama, they do have a rich store of traditions that indicate a Jewish heritage. From cooking traditions that conform to kosher dietary laws ("An egg with a blood spot was always thrown away.") to markings on the right side of the door that look eerily like the Hebrew letter *"shin"* which appears even today on the traditional mezuzah case, to special marriage blessings that take place *sotto la coperta*, under a special crocheted covering reminiscent of the *chuppah*, the Jewish wedding canopy, Emma's family traditions place her squarely among the *"b'nei anusim"*. Emma is proud to count herself among those Italians whose families have only remnants of Jewish belief and practice but who have passed these traditions from family to family for generations.

"I know I am a Jew," says Emma who expressed her joy at learning that a rabbi in a synagogue near to her home had recently dedicated himself to welcoming *b'nei anusim* into traditional congregations. But as she began her return to her Jewish heritage, Emma was faced with what she felt were disheartening prejudices. Although she and her son studied for years and made formal conversion, the rabbi seemed dissatisfied. He complained that she lacked formal documentation of a matrilineal Jewish line, something that few a*nusim* can produce. Then there were discussions that indicated that synagogue officials were skeptical of her family's Jewish traditions, a situation that made Emma feel unwelcome in the community.

In fact the international organization *Kulanu* (Hebrew for "all of us") that represents lost and isolated Jewish communities worldwide is so concerned that they encourage Tisha B'Av observances to recognize and reverse what *anusim* often face. They write, "We at Kulanu encourage you to remember the rippling effects of the Inquisition ... Sadly not all synagogues give a warm welcome to returning *anusim*."

Emma's synagogue experience offers a real-life example of what Kulanu warns against. When she confronted the rabbi, he explained the reasoning behind his reluctance. He began by recounting Inquisition history, pointing out that in 1492 many Jews refused to convert to Christianity. The result was that entire families were burned alive (*autodafe`*) throughout Spain and Portugal and later in Sicily and in southern Italy. The rabbi went on to say that these were the real Jews and that the *anusim*, their descendants (who converted) chose an easier path. He added that while these forced converts maintained some Jewish traditions within their families, the rabbi intimated that their Judaism was suspect in that they did not live openly as Jews.

Technically, the rabbi is correct. The Jews who refused conversion remained Jewish even as their bodies went up in flames. The Jews who chose to convert to Christianity rather than submit to murderers were in no position to profess their Judaism in public. Instead they took their traditions underground. At great personal sacrifice and with great courage, these anusim practiced in secret. Emma's ancestors deserve appreciation and respect. They found a way to live as Jews.

On December 8, 2009, Rabbi Stephen Leon, rabbi for 24 years to *b'nei anusim* in the Southwest USA, introduced a resolution to the United Synagogues of Conservative Judaism (USCJ) at their Biennial Convention. This resolution, passed by acclamation, included the following acknowledgement and tribute to *b'nei anusim*:

"Whereas the fast day of Tisha B'Av recalls the very Hebrew date upon which the Jews of Spain were expelled from their country in 1492 and Whereas many Jews were forcibly converted to Christianity publicly but then continued to practice Judaism in secret... Be It Resolved ... to welcome the B'nai Anusim to Judaism and to welcome them into their congregations."

Today in Italy mainstream traditional Jewish communities profess the same welcome. Several conferences have been organized to acknowledge and celebrate the relationship between Tisha B'Av and how its theme should include openness to *anusim*. In fact, Renzo Gattegna, an elected president of UCEI, the Union of Italian Jewish Communities, recently led a professional meeting on the topic in Reggio Calabria and later wrote that the lost Jewish communities of southern Italy should be acknowledged without prejudice.

In Italian we have a saying, *sega la segatura*. Translated literally it means, "to saw the sawdust", and figuratively it implies that we Italians prefer talk to action. Resolutions, articles and pronouncements aside, *b'nei anusim* like Emma and like so many others throughout the south of Italy are eager to discover and embrace their Jewish roots. And like Emma they are genuinely confused when the so-called welcome is dampened by suspicion, skepticism and ridiculous demands for genealogical documentation that synagogue and community officials already know could not possibly exist.

It was Frederich Nietzsche who put it best when he wrote, "What doesn't kill you makes you strong." With experiences like Emma's, many Italian *b'nei anusim* understand what Nietzsche was talking about. And strength is exactly what Emma and so many others like her will need as they attempt to break the barriers that continue to rob them of their Judaism and victimize them yet again.

NOTE: Rabbi Barbara Aiello is a Bat Anusim and founder, in 2006, of Sinagoga Ner Tamid del Sud (The Eternal Light of the South. The pluralistic synagogue is open to Jewish of all backgrounds. Rabbi Barbara recently welcomed Emma into her community and officiated at the Bar Mitzvah of Emma's son, Alessandro.

Dalidà

The "Barbra Streisand" of Europe with Calabrian Jewish Roots

Although she was born Iolanda Cristina Gigliotti, when it came time to select a stage name, she chose "Dalidà", from the Hebrew for "delight". And, as Dalidà she became one of the world's most beloved performers, singing and recording in more than ten languages, including Hebrew.

What is Dalidà's Calabrian Jewish connection? Her parents, Pietro and Giuseppina were born in my Calabrian town of Serrastretta. Their surname "Gigliotti", is a local name that is recognized as Jewish from Inquisition times. In addition it was "Nonno Enrico", Dalidà's grandfather, who professed Algerian Jewish roots – all of which lead to Dalidà's place of honor in the hearts of Calabrian Jews and of *b'nei anusim* everywhere.

Dalidà was born in Egypt after her parents settled there, a move they made so that her father could pursue his career as a concert violinist. Dalidà spent her early years in Egypt's bustling Italian Egyptian community but she lived most of her adult life in France.

Dalidà career spanned 30 years with a debut in 1956 and a final recording in 1986, just months before her untimely death. Known throughout Europe and Asia for her sultry voice and thoughtful lyrics, Dalidà is credited for bringing the first ethnic fusion hit to the contemporary music scene. *"Salma ya Salama"*, based on a traditional Egyptian folk song, was translated into French, Italian and German and sung around the world.

American appreciation of Dalidà soared after her critically acclaimed Broadway-themed show at Carnegie Hall in New York City but we *Serrastrettesi* remember her for the concert she brought to her home town in the 1970's.

Dalidà's performance of *Hava Nagila* earned her acclaim early in her career. When asked about why she chose a Hebrew melody, Dalidà told the audience that the melody was in her blood.

Each year on her Yahrzeit, the date of her passing, (May 3, 1987) the Serrastretta community remembers Dalidà. Our local cultural society,

Associazione Dalidà, often organizes a concert in her memory in an outdoor theatre that bears her name, while a museum exhibit at *Casa Museo Dalidà* chronicles her life. Recently the Dalidà restaurant was renovated and opened to the public. The menu features traditional Calabrian dishes served while diners listen to Dalidà`s more famous melodies.

As the Italian Jewish Cultural Center in Calabria continues to discover and establish our ancient Jewish presence here in the south of Italy, we are honored to claim the beloved Dalidà as one of our own. One of our *bat anusim* ladies put it so well. "Dalidà, the Barbra Streisand of Europe, Dalidà was *i nostri* - she was one of us."

We Are Not "Diet Coke!"

A Pluralistic Jewish Lament

As the first and only woman rabbi and non-orthodox rabbi in Italy, I am often asked to explain the differences between modern pluralistic Judaism and the more traditional approach to Jewish belief and practice. From my very first year in Italy (2004) when I was appointed rabbi at Italy's first non-orthodox synagogue in Milan, the population in general, as well as specific groups, from journalists to Jews, wanted to know how this modern approach to Judaism interfaces with orthodoxy – the only branch of Judaism that Italy has ever known.

At first I was given to long explanations where I would try to weave theology with history and history with heritage – all in Italian, which is not my *madre lingua*.

Oy vey-issimo! As my discourses became more complicated and as my audiences and I became more frustrated, it was a young lady, a guest at a wedding where I was the officiant, who turned things around, helping me discover a unique way to explain denominational differences.

The wedding ceremony was held in a gorgeous setting – on the grounds of a villa that bordered Lake Como in the north of Italy. The bride, a Jewish girl from Milan was marrying her beloved, a young man from a Catholic family. When I first met Rubina, I was impressed with her determination to incorporate both faith traditions into the ceremony and I was honored and delighted to help this couple who so very much wanted to invite God into their interfaith partnership.

On a lovely Sunday evening we three stood under the *chuppah* - the Jewish bride, the Catholic groom and the modern woman rabbi! The ceremony itself was *meravigliosa!* Wonderful! It included the traditional bridal canopy, the *kiddushin* blessing, the *Shevah Brachot* (seven wedding blessings where the bride circles the groom) and the *ketubah*, the Jewish wedding document that the couple designed to celebrate the mutual respect they had for their partner's faith. Readings included Bible passages from the Book of Psalms and Proverbs, which were part of the groom's Catholic traditions, along with an instrumental version of *Ave Maria*. Of course, the ceremony concluded with the breaking of the glass.

But it was at the wedding reception when I was confronted by one of the bride's close friends, that I truly understood how important it is to clearly define the differences between traditional and modern streams of Judaism. The guest's comment enlightened me when, after she thanked me for the beautiful ceremony, she went on to say, "I didn't expect to see anything Jewish at this wedding." When I asked her why she thought that way, the young woman said, "Well, you are a woman rabbi, something that is not permitted. You have broken all the Jewish rules. I heard that you make Shabbat in five minutes, that you don't ever read Torah and that at the Passover seder you serve lobster!"

That's when I knew. The orthodox community in Milan, and later as I observed, in most of Italy has the misconception that their brand of Judaism is "Coca Cola", while we modern pluralistic Jews aren't the real thing. We're the "Diet Coke" of Italian Judaism!

Attribute it to fear of the unknown, fear of change, fear of losing a level of comfort or security, but the perception that a modern approach is necessarily a watered down version of Jewish tradition is something that I now work hard to dispel.

Jewish law, *halakah* as it is called in Hebrew, derives from the Hebrew root, *holech* which means "to walk". This relationship strongly implies that Jewish law is ever changing, adapting with the times, or, as the 15th century Rabbi Isserles put it, "Halakah must always be based upon new knowledge."

So as we modern Italian Jews do our *"holech-ing"*, or as we walk the path of progress, we incorporate new knowledge into existing Jewish tradition. Specifically that means that we study Jewish dietary laws and learn about establishing and maintaining a kosher kitchen. Then we modern Jews make personal choices about the food we eat, secure in the knowledge that if we maintain a strictly kosher diet, we know why we do it and if we do not keep kosher, we have made an informed choice as to why we do not.

Today an informed public understands that homosexuality is not a "life style choice", but as biologists have speculated and as Lady Gaga emphasizes, people with gender differences are likely "born that way". Given this new knowledge, modern Judaism openly welcomes gay and lesbian Jews as well as their partners and their children.

Rashi, said to be Judaism's greatest commentator, pointed out that there was never a prohibition that stated that women could not read Torah, lay *tfillin* or participate in prayer service and Talmudic studies. Rashi and others emphasized that women were "exempt" from these *mitzvot* given their responsibilities at home. Over the years this exemption became a prohibition.

As modern pluralistic Jews we examine our history to verify the value of women's participation. Now our women are free to become rabbis, to read Torah, and to become a Bat Mitzvah with the same level of participation as is required of her male Bar Mitzvah counterparts.

If my wedding guest were to visit our modern synagogue, Ner Tamid del Sud, on a Friday evening or a Saturday morning, she would feel *Jewishly* quite a home. Like the traditionalists, we light the Shabbat candles, make all the blessings in Hebrew, sing the Shabbat melodies and on Saturday mornings, we read from the Torah scroll. At a recent Bar Mitzvah service in our synagogue, Alessandro Yosef wrapped tfillin and, using an ancient Italian trope, chanted directly from our 1783 Torah scroll. And then we all enjoyed a kosher *kiddush* lunch.

It's been over a decade that I've served as rabbi here in Italy and I've learned so much. I've come to understand and respect a traditional approach to Judaism while at the same time I am able to offer an open and welcoming opportunity to those Jews who appreciate the incorporation of modernity and relevancy into Jewish belief and practice.

How does that translate? Very well, especially since I now begin my lectures with two familiar bottles, one in each hand. "If Judaism is Coca Cola," I say to my audience, "I am here to explain to you how modern pluralistic Judaism, is grounded in Jewish tradition. Instead of Diet Coke, we modern Italian Jews are just like our traditional brothers and sisters. Both of us are "the real thing".

Rabbi Akiva's Message

A Perfect Lesson for Sicily's B'nei Anusim

I board the train at the station in Lamezia Terme, the biggest town closest to my mountain village in Calabria, and head toward another town, Villa San Giovanni. There the train, with all the passengers on board, will itself board a ferry boat, taking us cross the Straits of Messina to the island of Sicily. My train will continue north where I will greet the members of our modern pluralistic *chavurah*, Ner Tamid Palermo.

Or what's left of them.

As the Lag B'Omer festival approaches, I'm feeling a little like Rabbi Akiva these days. Akiva was the sage whose 24,000 students all died during the period of the *Omer*. A mysterious disease killed them and it was only on *Lag B'Omer* (the 33rd day) that the dying stopped, hence the reason for the joyful celebration that continues to this day.

What killed them all? According to Rebbetzin Tziporah Heller (Aish.com *"Lag B'Omer: The Beauty in Every Jew"*), "The Sages say that they did not treat each other with *kavod* – respect – and therefore they were stricken with a disease that caused them to choke to death." Heller goes on to explain the origins of the Hebrew word *"kavod"*, and how it relates to the word that shares its same Hebrew letters – the word, "heavy". Heller postulates that this heaviness implies recognizing another person, in particular another Jew, as significant. Heller believes, and I concur, that quite possibly Rabbi Akiva's students refused to acknowledge that every Jew has value. So what happened? They began to choke, and gasping for air, nearly all of them died. How ironic, especially since, as Heller puts it, "failing to give proper respect to another person means ceasing to take in *ruach* – spirit. When a person does not honor another Jew, it shows that he has stopped appreciating that person's unique spirit."

What's important here is that although Rabbi Akiva's yeshiva was decimated, he didn't give up. In fact he found five new students and started all over again. As I prepare for my journey to Palermo, Akiva's message rings true. I am travelling to rekindle the spirit of a decimated Jewish community – brought down not by

43

disease but by the confusion caused by Jews creating havoc within a holy Jewish community.

As founder of the *B'nei Anusim* movement in Calabria and Sicily, I had the joy and honor to bring to the island of Sicily, ancestral home of thousands of secret Jews, the first Passover *seder* in 500 years since Inquisition times. The *seder* and the *chavurah* that resulted from that effort happened nearly 10 years ago. During those years our small congregation, Ner Tamid Palermo grew to support the first public Bar Mitzvah in Sicily when our lay leader read from the Torah scroll to the delight of more than 50 members and friends.

Our liberal pluralistic Jewish community continued to thrive until traditionalists arrived to convince our fragile group that it was now time for them to leave the woman rabbi (insulted by some in two languages as a *"shonda"* and a *"scandolo"*) and become "authentic" Jews. Some succumbed to the pressure (If you can't beat 'em, join 'em) and now I, like Akiva will begin again.

These days it is not necessary for us to understand that an *"omer"* is an ancient unit of measure related to a barely stalk. Instead we must internalize what the custom implies. In these days when denominational differences spark vitriolic comments, anger and resentment among Jews of varied backgrounds and persuasions, the little festival of Lag B'Omer is a spiritual alarm clock, our divine wake-up call. As another rabbi once said, "On Lag B'Omer God saved the Jewish people to remind us that there is only one thing worse than the oppression of Jews by others. It is the oppression that one Jew does to another through gossip, slander and disrespect." Lag B'Omer exists to remind us of the importance of treating all of our Jewish brothers and sisters with love and tolerance, appreciation and, *kavod.*

"Cavalluccio" in Italian is "Piggyback"

After Ten Years Work by the Modern Jewish Movement,

Orthodox Rabbis "Discover" Italian B'nei Anusim

Charles Caleb Cotton said it first, "Imitation is the highest form of flattery." But it is the orthodox Jews who have come to the deep south of Italy who put Cotton's words into action. The *B'nei Anusim* movement in Calabria and Sicily that orthodox rabbis describe as a "new" initiative actually began more than ten years ago and has grown each year since. As rabbi for two *b'nei anusim* communities and founder of Italy's *B'nei Anusim* movement, we have an exciting story to tell – a story which encompasses our hard work and includes those who have attempted to usurp our efforts and call them their own.

The date was **December 5, 2004** and I found myself in a place not often frequented by a Jewish rabbi – the salon of a Catholic Church. I had just concluded a lecture on the lost Jews of Sicily and Calabria when a young woman pushed her way forward, through the crowd that had gathered around me.

Monsignor Natale Colafati, who was now directing this animated group of Calabresi to a side room, provided the impetus for this historic meeting. Opening the Calabrian church to my lecture *"La Judeka di Nicastro e la Storia degli Ebrei"*("The Jewish Quarter of Nicastro and the History of the Jews"), the Monsignor introduced my presentation by reminding the audience of more than 100 Calabresi how important it is to understand one's history. To my right on the dais sat a renowned professor, Vincenzo Villella, whose book about the Jews of Nicastro was one of only a very few volumes that acknowledged the ancient historical presence of the Jews in Calabria.

Even though my *"lingua italiana"* left much to be desired, the audience sat in rapt attention, completely absorbed by my family's story. When the lecture concluded, I was stunned by the number of local Calabresi who wanted to know more. That's when the young woman demanded my attention. She grabbed my hand and whispered, "I have always felt Jewish but no ever believed that our family could be Jewish. Please help me."

Her name was Antonella and when she told me her surname, I recognized it at once as one of many surnames listed in the Inquisition records that I had uncovered – names that indicated strong Jewish ancestry. Pressing Antonella's hand between my own, I promised her that I would help her. It was that promise that formed the basis of what was to become a ten year study of the thriving Jewish population that once graced hundreds of Calabrian villages and towns and a personal mission to serve those who wanted to know more.

As the first woman and first modern Pluralistic rabbi in Italy, I had returned to Calabria, the land of my roots, where I had organized what was to become the first and only initiative to help southern Italians discover and embrace something that had been hidden from them for nearly 500 years. I had come to help them find their own Jewish roots.

In Hebrew we say, *"b'nei anusim"*, a phrase that means "the children of the forced ones". Forced? How? More than 500 years ago, during the time of the Inquisition our ancestors were forced to do one of two things; we were forced to either abandon our Jewish religion and submit to forced conversion, or we were expelled from our homes and villages.

As a *"bat anusim"* (daughter of the forced ones), I have personal experience with this tragedy. My own ancestors, Spanish Jews, were forced to flee Toledo, Spain, then to Portugal, then to Sicily and finally to the mountains of Calabria to escape persecution, arrest or death.

In fact, my great grandmother, Angela Rosa Grande was a direct descendant of Matheo de Grande, a *neofite* or "New Christian", whose property and goods were confiscated by the Inquisition authorities in the Sicilian town of Naro. The family was arrested for "Judaizing", or practicing their Jewish traditions in secret. Finally settling in the tiny mountain village they called Serrastretta, my ancestors found a place to be Jewish, but given their frightening experiences, they chose to continue their clandestine observance. For centuries they lit candles on Friday evening, abstained for eating pork and, when a loved one died, they sat on low chairs and covered the mirrors throughout the house, ancient Jewish traditions they practice to this day.

On **November 10, 2005** – *Associazione per la ricerca e lo studio sugli Ebrei in Calabria e Sicilia,* (The Association for the research and study of the Jews of Calabria and Sicily) was born. Officers Dominick Porto, historian Vincenzo Villella and demographer Enrico Mascaro spearheaded the effort and pledged to organize events to promote the Jewish history and traditions of the southern Italy, a promise they continue to take very seriously.

Thanks to a grant in 2006 by the Vuolo -Bernstein Foundation, a philanthropic group that supports Italian Jewish heritage, we were able to expand our efforts to include lectures, workshops and classes for Calabrians who were curious about their family's Jewish roots. We continue our work to connect Calabrians and Sicilians with their lost Jewish traditions in an effort that has become a ten year labor of love.

Specifically the History of the *b'nei anusim* movement in Calabria and Sicily is as follows:

2003
Intense research begins in Calabria and Sicily as stories of Jewish family traditions emerge from southern Italians in villages scattered throughout the *Meridionale.*

2004
Calabria - Lamezia Terme - Rabbi Barbara Aiello, first modern rabbi in Italy, delivers the first *b'nei anusim* lecture, "La Judeka di Nicrasto e la Storia degli Ebrei". (The Jewish Quarter of Nicastro and the History of the Jews)

2005
Calabria, Lamezia Terme – *Associazione per la ricerca e lo studio sugli Ebrei in Calabria e Sicilia,* (The Association for the research and study of the Jews of Calabria and Sicily) is registered with the Italian government.

Piano Battaglia, Sicily and Serrastretta, Calabria – the Pluralistic Jewish movement leads the first public Passover seders in 500 years.

Bova Marina, Calabria – Pluralistic movement researchers visit the ancient synagogue excavation and initiate a campaign to publicize this remarkable find.

2006

The Vuolo -Bernstein Foundation provides seed money to fund the *B'nei Anusim* movement.

Dedication of synagogue Ner Tamid del Sud ("The Eternal Light of the South"), sometimes called "The Calabria Synagogue", the first active synagogue in Calabria in 500 years since Inquisition times.

American anusim couple, Andy and Lupe are married in a Jewish ceremony at the ruins of the castle of King Frederick II. The castle overlooks *Timpone*, an ancient Jewish Quarter where Jews were offered protection from persecution. In this historic ceremony, the first Jewish wedding in 500 years, local Italian *b'nei anusim* held the chuppah high above the bride and groom.

2007

Synagogue Ner Tamid del Sud, The Calabrian Synagogue, hosts the first Bar Mitzvah in Calabria in 500 years.

In Selinunte, Sicily *anusim* celebrate Passover with the ancient "Seder *Hamishi*", a historic meal with prayers and blessings, held on the fifth night of Passover. The Seder *Hamishi* commemorates the secret meal hosted by Sicilian Christians who opened their homes to local Jews on the fifth night of Passover so that their Jewish neighbors could celebrate undetected by Inquisition authorities.

The Calabria Synagogue hosts the first ever Shabbaton study weekend for *b'nei anusim* to study the Hebrew language, kosher traditions and Jewish belief and pracice.

At the first public celebration of Chanukah in Calabria in 500 years, Rabbi Aiello instructs 45 *b'nei anusim* on the lighting of the Chanukah candles.

2008

Calabria, Cosenza, Ferramonti Deportation Camp – meetings and lectures to increase awareness of the role of the Italian soldiers and local citizens in saving more than 3,000 Jews.

The Italian Jewish Cultural Center of Calabria (The IjCCC,) hosts the first Italian Jewish Roots Conference.

2009

The Italian Jewish Cultural Center of Calabria (IjCCC) hosts the second Italian Jewish Roots Conference featuring Rabbi Aiello, Professor Enrico Tromba, archaeologist for the Bova Marina excavation and Jewish DNA expert, Bennett Greenspan. More than 100 attendees gather to learn how to discover and embrace their lost Jewish roots.

2010

Rabbi Aiello is commencement speaker at the American University at Rome and is honored for her work as founder of the *B'nei Anusim* movement in Calabria and Sicily.

The Calabria Synagogue welcomes the first Bat Mitzvah in Calabria who becomes the first girl in Calabrian history to read directly from the Torah scroll.

2011

In Palermo, Sicily, Rabbi Aiello officiates at the Bar Mitzvah of lay leader Salvo Parrucca – first *anusim* and first public Bar Mitzvah ceremony in 500 years.

2012

Rabbi Aiello's pioneering work with *b'nei anusim* is featured in the Canadian documentary, "The Secret of San Nicandro".

The IjCCC delivers a Torah scroll to Chavurah Ner Tamid Palermo, the first modern pluralistic congregation in Sicily.

Ner Tamid del Sud community member Alessandro Yosef becomes the first *anusim* student to become Bar Mitzvah in Calabria.

2013

Rabbi Barbara Aiello and the *b'nei anusim* Calabria community are recognized at the International Holocaust Memorial Day, hosted by the Italian Consulate on January 27, 2013 in Tampa, Florida.

Italian newspapers report that orthodox rabbis have just "discovered" the southern Italian *b'nei anusim*!

2014

Launch of the new book by Professor Vincenzo Villella, *Giudecce di Calabria –* (The Jewish Neighborhoods of Calabria) which features dozens of Calabrian villages where Jewish life once flourished.

2015

Premiere of the film documentary, "The Secret Jews of Calabria", held at the historic Brotherhood Synagogue in New York City. The film features Rabbi Barbara and her work with b'nei anusim - hidden Calabrian Jews

*****

Throughout our twelve year journey, our cultural center and synagogue has organized Shabbat services, festival celebrations, lectures, concerts and workshops and individual studies designed to illuminate the path for lost and isolated Jews of southern Italy who long to find and learn about their lost Jewish heritage.

For more than a decade the synagogue and cultural center have been central to the Pluralistic Jewish movement that offers a modern approach to Jewish belief and practice. For years now we have extended the hand of Jewish welcome to all those whose personal history propels them to our door.

We are egalitarian in that we offer the opportunity to all women to participate equally in the services and festivals. We do not separate women from men and any woman who desires to do so may touch, carry or read directly from the Torah scroll.

We open our hearts to interfaith families, in that we do not force the non-Jewish partner to make conversion – our personal histories, dating back to Inquisition times, affirm that forced conversions are always problematic and never appropriate.

We accept as Jewish the children of Jewish fathers as well as Jewish mothers and we welcome gay and lesbian individuals, couples and their children who can live openly as both gay and Jewish.

Interestingly enough, in less than one year traditional rabbis, along with an Israeli based organization have come to Calabria and Sicily to "discover" the *anusim*. In news articles and televised interviews my orthodox colleagues breathlessly relate how they have just now found these lost Jews.

In Italian we have a word for this. It's called *cavalluccio,* which in English, means "piggyback". After years of dogged effort by the modern Jewish movement, my *cavalluccio* colleagues have given us a high compliment by attempting to co-opt those efforts and pass them off as their own.

Yet our mission remains the same. We will continue on our path to celebrate the deep Jewish roots of Calabria and Sicily's *b'nei anusim.* In addition we will offer the traditional rabbis and Jewish community leaders who have descended upon us from outside Calabria and Sicily and who attempt to establish themselves as the only point of authentic *anusim* reference – we will offer those who *"giocano cavalluccio"*, (who play piggyback) the opportunity to share in our knowledge, our culture and our experience that, in more than ten years, is credible, extensive and not to be ignored.

The Jews Can Save Columbus Day

Columbus' Crypto- Jewish Heritage Makes Him One of Us

"In Fourteen Hundred and Ninety-Two…" Everyone can finish the first line of the famous poem with "Columbus sailed the ocean blue."

The Columbus poem, whose official title is "The History of the U. S.," was written by Winifred Sackville Stoner, Jr., a child prodigy whose mother pioneered the Natural Education Movement, an innovative pedagogy designed to make learning fun. Using rhyming couplets to remember important facts, little Winnie, Jr. penned the poem whose first two lines almost any American can recite.

But it's not just Winnie's poem that celebrates the famous explorer. Columbus Day was celebrated unofficially as early as the 18th century and finally became a federal holiday in 1937. Yet, even though the poem ends with the disclaimer, "The first American? No, not quite. But Columbus was brave, and he was bright," a number of groups nationwide want the holiday abolished. Some would like to deep six Columbus Day and replace it with one that recalls that Native Americans were here first and didn't need discovering, thank you very much.

Anthony J. Baratta, National President of the Order of the Sons of Italy in America feels differently. In a recent memo to OSIA members, Baratta writes, "More than five hundred years ago, a strong man with an unmistakably Italian name took a world divided in half and made it whole. When Cristoforo Colombo crossed a huge, dark ocean, he joined the Old World of Europe to the New World of what was to become America. His voyage changed the world forever."

Opponents would agree but not for the same reasons. For example, Nadra Kareem Nittle in an article "The Argument Against Columbus Day", writes "…the Italian explorer's arrival in the New World ushered in genocide against indigenous peoples as well as the transatlantic slave trade." Nittle and others feel the holiday should be abolished.

So as the argument rages on, I propose a solution. Since Columbus was most likely an Italian Jew, organizations that represent these two minorities could join forces and celebrate Columbus for the hero that he was – an Italian Jewish explorer whose devotion to Judaism impacted lives and saved many. Yes, Columbus was Jewish.

In a 2012 CNN opinion piece Charles Garcia summarized what historians had long suspected and recently corroborated – that Cristobol Colon` was a secret Jew, a *marrano*, who worked to save his fellow Jews from the horrors of persecution brought on by the Inquisition authorities who were determined to rid Spain of its Jewish population.

Garcia tells us that, according to Spanish historians and scholars, among them Jose Erugo, Celso Garcia de la Riega and Otero Sanchez, along with British historian, Cecil Roth and linguistics expert Estelle Irizarry, Columbus wrote and spoke in Castilian Spanish or Ladino that was the "Yiddish" of 15th century Spanish Jews. Columbus used Hebrew words and phrases in his correspondence, among them a Hebrew blessing meaning "with God's help", that most Spanish Jews used as well.

But it was Columbus' actions that merit the most praise. At the time that he set sail, Jews routinely suffered horrible persecutions at the hands of the authorities of the Spanish Inquisition. Under threat of arrest and torture, Jews were forced to accept Christian conversion. Those who refused were often rounded up, driven to the center of town, tied to posts and burned alive. Thousands were driven from Spain after their homes were looted their businesses burned and their livelihood destroyed.

In his book, "Sails of Hope", Simon Wiesenthal wrote about Columbus' motivation for his voyages. Ironically, Wiesenthal writes that Columbus ultimately wanted to stem the tide of Jewish genocide by finding a safe haven for his Jewish brothers and sisters.

October 12, 1492 is important for two reasons. Obviously that was the day that Columbus set sail. What is not as well known is that October 12, 1492 was also the exact same date that Spanish Jews were, by law, given the choice of accepting forced conversion, leaving Spain or, if they remained they could be arrested, tortured and eventually murdered.

Charles Garcia concludes that "As we witness bloodshed the world over in the name of religious freedom, it is valuable to take another look at the man who sailed the seas in search of such freedoms – landing in a place that would eventually come to hold such an ideal at its very core."

I agree. Columbus Day can be saved and given this man's remarkable history, it seems that we Italian Jews are uniquely positioned to do just that.

A Christmas Conundrum

An American Rabbi in Catholic Italy

Even here in Italy it's headline news that public Christmas celebrations in the US are under siege. But the cream in the cannoli (Italy's version of "the icing on the cake"), is that a US military base has been forced to dismantle the entire nativity scene and unceremoniously boot it off government property.

"Che fa?", "What's up with that?" ask my Italian friends who want to know how I, as an American Jew, and a rabbi no less, feel about a Christmas tradition that is ubiquitous in Italy but almost banned completely at home.

I have been living and working in Italy for more than a decade, mostly in Serrastretta, a tiny village in Calabria near the "toe" of the Italian "boot". As the rabbi of a small pluralistic synagogue and the first and only woman rabbi in Italy, I'm a double whammy minority in a country where Christian traditions abound.

The main event in our village and in hundreds of others throughout Italy is the nativity scene. These dioramas are called *presepe* (pronounced "pray-seh-pay") and during the month of December they proliferate from north to south. There are competitions to see who can make the most creative manger scene. In fact, a first place contender stands in front of a local public high school where art students have created life-size mannequins of Mary, Joseph, the shepherds and the Three Kings and dressed them in historically accurate costumes.

Beginning at Christmas week these scenes become even more elaborate when the *presepe vivente* are all the rage. These are nativity scenes with live actors and real animals and, if there's been a birth in town, there's a real "baby Jesus" in the manger.

As one of the few Jews in the area, I am often asked (mostly by American ex-pats) how I feel about this Christmas practice that has caused such a stir at home. "Does the Nativity offend you?" they ask. I respond, "No, not at all."

As a Jew I hold Jesus in esteem (after all Jesus was born, lived and died a Jew) and I am grateful to him for sharing and living the Torah principles that he learned as child. For this reason, among others, most Jews I know do not dislike Christmas. Even though Jews don't observe the holiday, we are glad that Christians do. Throughout my growing up years in the US, and now as a Jew in Italy, I can say to my Christian friends that I truly enjoy being a guest at your party.

It's a lesson I learned as a child and recently repeated by American rabbis - my parents taught me the difference between my own birthday party and someone else's. It's a simple lesson that I apply today to the deluge of Italian Christmas celebrations all around me. It's someone else's party, not mine.

The lights, the carols, the tree and the nativities indicate that I am a guest who is included in the celebration. I am a polite guest who does not whine, complain or demand that the celebrants take down the decorations, stop the singing and curtail the festivities because it's not my day. Instead, like most children have learned to do, I share in the joy of someone else's special celebration.

Here in southern Italy, "Christ" is still the Christmas headline and that's fine with me. In fact, for many of my Calabrian neighbors, the baby Jesus' message of peace, love and harmony is the focus of December 25. Not the presents.

Gifts arrive on January 6, brought by *La Befana*, a dear old lady who flies through the air on a broomstick and leaves surprises in the shoes that the children have placed outside the door the night before. Interestingly, *La Befana* represents an important physical separation between the spiritual message of Christmas and the material aspects of the season – a concept that, as a rabbi, I fully support.

As Rabbi Joseph Telushkin wrote in his book, "Jewish Literacy," each Christmas season we can wish all of our Christian friends the joys of their holiday, "especially since Jesus' message was one of peace, understanding and love – the very same things we Jews pray for in our synagogues and work toward in our communities." The songs, decorations, and especially the Italian nativity scenes emphasize this to a troubled world. As a Jew, I applaud the Christmas celebration and appreciate the opportunity to be a guest at the party.

An Italian Midrash

Il Cappotto del Rabbino – The Rabbi's Coat

L'inverno e' stato lungo e freddo nel piccolo paese di montagna sopra Torino.

The winters were long and cold in the little village high up on a mountain above Turin.

Qualche volta la neve ha cominciato in settembre ed e' rimasta fino a maggio!

Sometimes the snow began in September and stayed on the ground until May.

Ma il rabbino e' giovane, pieno di energia, e per lui il tempo brutto non fa niente.

But the rabbi was young and energetic and the brutal weather didn't bother him at all.

Ogni giorno la gente ha visto lui... col cavallo e il calesse ... viaggiare nella campagna a far visita alle sue famiglie ebree.

Because every day his neighbors could see him, with his horse and wagon, traveling into the country to visit his Jewish families.

Gli ebrei in paese volevano molto bene al loro rabbino.

The Jews in the village loved their rabbi.

E per questo hanno voluto fare qualcosa di speciale per lui.

And so they wanted to do something very special for him.

Uno ha detto: "La cosa buona per il nostro rabbino e' un nuovo calesse"

One person said, "A good thing for our rabbi is a new wagon!"

"No... no," ha detto un altro. Il calesse costa troppo. Non abbiamo i soldi per quello."

"No, no," said another. A wagon costs too much. We don't have money for that."

"Va ben... va ben... io voglio comprare un cavallo. Con il cavallo piu' giovane sarebbe possibile per il nostro rabbino viaggare piu' presto... e di non stare fuori nel vento freddo."

"OK, OK, but I want to buy a horse. With a younger horse, our rabbi could travel faster and he wouldn't spend so much time out in the cold wind."

Ma la gente non ha avuto soldi per un cavallo.

But the villagers did not have money for horse either.

Ma, un giorno, dopo lo Shabbat, il sarto ha cercato la gente. Ha parlato sottovoce perche' non ha voluto che il rabbino sentisse.

But one day, after Shabbat, the tailor approached his friends. He spoke in a whisper... like this, so the Rabbi would not hear.

"Io ho un'idea. Ho notato che il rabbino ha un cappotto vecchio... brutto."

"I have an idea. I noticed that the rabbi's coat is old and worn..."

"Ho fatto cappotti per trent'anni. La gente dice che i miei cappotti sono piu'confortevoli, piu' caldi degli altri... Io faro' un cappotto bellissimo per il nostro rabbino!"

"I have made coats for thirty years. The people say that my coats are warmer than any other... I will make a beautiful coat for our rabbi."

La gente e' stata contentissima di questa idea. Insieme, hanno raccolto i loro soldi e hanno comperato la stoffa di lana ... perfetta..

The people were very happy with this idea so together they collected their money and bought a perfect piece of wool.

E dei soldi sono rimasti... hanno anche comperato un pezzo di pelle per rivestire il collo del cappotto."

They collected so much money that they had some left over so they bought a nice piece of fur to make a hat as well.

Finalmente, dopo tre mesi, quando l'inverno ha cominciato a far sentire il suo rigore, il sarto ha finito il cappotto.

Finally, after three months, just as winter was approaching, the tailor finished the coat.

E' stato di venerdi' sera, prima dello Shabbat, quando il rabbino ha sentito bussare alla sua porta.

It was Friday evening, just before Shabbat, when the rabbi heard a knock on his door.

Davanti a lui si e' presentato il gruppo dei suoi amici... Hanno gridato: "Rav, abbiamo una sorpresa grande per te!"

In front of him stood a group of his friends. They shouted, "Rabbi, we have a big surprise for you."

Sono entrati in casa e hanno dato il cappotto al rabbino. E' stato perfetto per lui.

And then they all trooped into the house and gave the rabbi his new coat. It was a perfect fit.

Per la prima volta nella sua vita, il rabbino non ha avuto una parole da dire...

For the first time in his life the Rabbi could not find a word to say...

Lui stava senza parole. Ha detto solo: "Ooooo... Ahhhhhh..."

Dopo un abbraccio per tutti, hugs all around... hanno cantato "Shehechianu..." Il rabbino ha detto:" Amici miei grandissimi, il vostro regalo e' perfetto e voi me lo avete dato al momento giusto..."

My dear friends, your gift is perfect and you have given it to me at a good time.

Domenica io comincero' un lungo viaggio.

Sunday I begin a long journey.

Ogni anno, prima che il tempo in 'inverno diventi molto brutto ma io andro' ai trovare mio fratello.

Every year, before the winter is at its worst, I go to visit my brother.

Lui abita su... molto in alto sulla montagna... sopra il nostro villaggio.

He lives high up in the mountain above our village.

E' vecchio ... ha vent'anni piu' di me ... Adesso e' debole e ammalato. Con il mio cappotto nuovo, il viaggio sara' piu' facile per me.

He is very old, actually twenty years older than I and now he is frail and ill. With my new coat, the journey will be easier for me.

Il viaggio a casa di suo fratello e' stato molto difficile. Il tempo era ormai cambiato e adesso faceva proprio molto freddo.

Indeed, the trip to his brother's house was very difficult. The weather had changed and now it was very cold.

La strada stretta e' stata piena di ghiaccio e ha dovuto camminare molto lentamente

The narrow road was full of ice which made the journey very slow.

Il vento e' stato fortissimo.

The wind was very strong.

Dopo tre settimana, finalmente, il rabbino e' arrivato a casa di suo fratello.

And after three weeks, finally the rabbi reached his brother's house.

Bussa alla porta...cosi'... He knocked on the door like this... *Niente!* Nothing.

Finalmente il rabbino ha aperto la porta e ha visto suo fratello sotto una coperta vecchia, davanti a un piccolo fuoco.

Finally the rabbi opened the door to see his brother under an old blanket, in front of a little fire.

La casa era fredda e buia, ma quando ha visto il rabbino suo fratello, la luce del sorriso ha riempito la stanza.

The house was cold and dark but when he saw the rabbi the light of the brother's smile filled the room.

La differenza d' eta fra i due fratelli e' stata grande, ma i due sono stati amici grandissimi e si son voluti bene l'un l'altro.

The difference in the ages of the two brothers was great but the two were the best of friends and loved each other dearly.

Ma in un momento, il rabbino ha visto qualcosa di molto strano perche' il suo fratello ha cambiato espressione..

But in a moment, the rabbi saw something so strange. His brother's expression changed abruptly.

E ha cominciato a piangere forte.

His brother began to cry and cry and cry.

"Fratello," il rabbino ha gridato, "Che e' successo? Perche' tu sei triste di vedermi? Dimmi, che cosa e' successo?"

The rabbi was stunned. "My brother, what has happened? Why are you so sad to see me? Tell me what bad thing I have done?"

Il fratello ha fatto cosi' e cosi' e ha detto, "Scusami. Io sono un vecchietto un po' pazzo. Dopo il tuo lungo viaggio, sono imbarazzato nel dire la cosa che ha portato le mie lacrime."

His brother said, "I am sorry. I am a such a crazy old man. I am embarrassed to tell you what made me cry."

Ma il rabbino ha insistito e finalmente il fratello si e' deciso di parlare.

But the rabbi continued to ask him and finally his brother relented.

Ha detto: "Mio fratellino carissimo, quando tu sei nato io ho avuto vent'anni.

My dearest little brother, when you were born, I was twenty years old.

Sono stato il primo figlio e poi, una sorella, sorella... sorella.. sorella...sorella.. sorella... sorella.

and then after me seven sisters... and then a brother for me!

finalmente un fratello per me!

I nostri genitori sono stati bravissimi, specialmente il nostro papa' ma e' morto quando tu eri un bimbo"

Our parents were wonderful, especially our father but he died when you were only a baby.

Ricordo che lui e' stato molto generoso. La nostra famiglia e' stata povera, ma sempre lui ha dato qualcosa a tutti.

I remember that he was very generous. Our family was very poor, but he always had something to give to everyone."

Un anno, quando la nostra gente ha guadagnato qualche soldo dopo aver venduto le verdure, e' andata nel villaggio- adesso il tuo villaggio.

One year, when the sale of vegetables had been especially good, the people went to a village- it was your village"

Li', hanno trovato un sarto famoso per fare un cappotto per nostro padre.

There they found a famous tailor to make a coat for our father.

Per questo mi sono commosso, ho pianto molto.

This is why I became so emotional and why I cried so much.

Tu, mio fratellino, tu sembri preciso il nostro papa'! Tu sei venuto da me con il cappotto identico a quello di nostro padre, preciso!"

My brother, you who look exactly like our father, came to me, wearing the exact same coat."

Il giovane rabbino rimase sorpreso nel sentire le parole di suo fratello. Mai aveva visto il suo papa' ma il rabbino ha sentito molto della generosita' la felicita' le "gimilut chassidim" che il papa' ha avuto per tutti e sempre ha provato di fare lo stesso.

The young rabbi was surprised to hear his brother's words. Although he never saw his father, he heard so much about his good deeds, called "gimlut chassidim" and so he always tried to live as he lived.

Ma il cuore del rabbino era rotto nel sentire il dolore di suo fratello. Ha pulito la casa, ha cucinato e ha aggiustato tutto per il fratello. Ma non ha parlato piu' del cappotto. Tutto e' stato a posto.

But it broke the rabbi's heart because he felt his brother's pain, so instead he cooked and cleaned and did not speak of the coat again. And everything was fine.

Durante il lungo viaggio di ritorno a casa, c'e' stato un temporale grande.

During the long journey home, there was a huge storm.

Quando il rabbino ha visto che il suo cavallo era stremato, si fermo' in una baita di contadini.

When his horse could go no further, the rabbi stopped at the home of a farm family.

La famiglia fu contentissima di dare ospitalita' al rabbino e prepararono tutte le cose buone per lui da mangiare.

The family was thrilled to offer their home to the rabbi. So they made him a wonderful meal.

La moglie preparo' una buona polenta, con fonduta e altri formaggi e anche una bagna cauda buonissima - tutto con formaggio e senza carne, per rispettare la legge kasher del rabbino.

The farmer's wife made a beautiful polenta, with a cheese fondue - everything with cheese, and no meat out of respect for the rabbi, who kept kosher.

Per dormire, hanno dato al rabbino un letto molto comodo e al mattino il rabbino si e' preparato per uscire.

They gave the rabbi the most comfortable bed to sleep in and in the morning the rabbi prepared to leave.

Il contadino ha detto: "C'e' una altra cosa che possiamo fare per te?"

The farmer asked the rabbi, "Can I do something else for you?"

Il rabbino ha pensato per un momento e poi ha detto: "Si`, io voglio cambiare il mio cappotto con il tuo."

The rabbi thought for a long minute then said, "Yes, I want to make a trade. I will give you my coat and you give me yours."

Il contatdino ha gridato, "No, mai! Il tuo cappotto e' bellissimo mentre il mio e' vecchio e piena di buchi."

The farmer shouted, "No never! Yours is a beautiful coat, while mine is old and full of holes."

Ma il rabbino ha insistito tanto e alla fine ha salutato con un lungo abbraccio il contadino, che adesso indossava il suo nuovo cappotto.

But the rabbi insisted and finally the rabbi gave a big hug to the farmer who was now dressed in the rabbi's beautiful coat.

Quando la gente del paese ha saputo questo del suo rabbino, sono stati arrabbiatissimi!

When the people in the rabbi's village heard this, they were very, very, very angry.

Hanno detto, "Com' e' possible che il nostro rabbino non abbia gratitudine per quello che noi abbiamo fatto per lui ?"

They said, "How can our rabbi be so ungrateful for what all of us did for him?"

Ma, durante Kabbalat Shabbat, il rabbino ha spiegato. The rabbi explained:

Ha raccontato la storia della memoria di suo fratello.

64

He told the story of how what his brother remembered, and then he said –e poi, a detto:

"Il vostro cappotto e' stato meraviglioso. Grazie, molte grazie, ma non e' possibile per voi sapere che il vostro regalo per me ha portato a mio fratello una grande memoria del nostro padre' Abbiamo ricordato la generosita' del nostro padre."

"My coat was wonderful and I thank you for it but you had no way of knowing that your gift to me would bring such strong memories to my brother. Memories of our father's generous spirit."

"Ma Dio mi ha chiesto di portare sempre lo spirito della generosita'.Ho avuto la potenza di fare la gioia della generosita' quando ho dato via il mio cappotto.

"God asks me to always bring with me the spirit of generosity. In my father's memory, I had the power to do that when I gave my coat away."

"Certo il cappotto ha portato il calore, ma il sorriso del contadino ha portato molto piu' calore "

"Certainly the coat brought me warmth, but nothing was warmer than that farmer's smile."

Il giorno di Kippur e' la nostra opportunita' di pensare alle cose che sono importanti per noi.

Yom Kippur is our opportunity to think about the things that are important to us.

Certamente non dobbiamo dar via i nostri cappotti, ma dobbiamo considerare le cose che sono piu' preziose.

Certainly we don't need to give our coats away, but we do need to consider the things that are most precious to us.

E come il rabbino della nostra storia, e' possibile decidere che i rapporti tra di noi sono piu' preziosi di ogni altra cosa..

And like the rabbi, we can decide that relationships are more important, more precious than anything we could ever have - even a wonderful coat.

Diciamo Let us say, Amen.

Zachor! Memories from Milan

My First Holocaust Memorial Day

January 27, 1945 marks the liberation of the Auschwitz death camp where one million Jews were murdered by the Nazis. Sixty years later, in November 2005 the United Nations General Assembly resolved that January 27 should be observed as a day to honor the memory of Holocaust victims and encourage the development of education programs about Holocaust history to help prevent further acts of genocide.

The calendar pages have turned and January 2015 marks my twelfth year as rabbi in Italy. I began my work in the north, in Milan, where I served Italy's first modern synagogue as Italy's first woman and first non-orthodox rabbi.

My father, Antonio Aiello (z"l) was a liberator of the Buchenwald death camp and his experiences, coupled with my living and working as I do as an Italian Jew on the "doorstep" of the Shoah, gave special significance to each January 27 – known throughout Europe as Holocaust Memorial Day.

One in particular touched my heart.

It was the morning of January 27, 2006 when Milan was paralyzed by the biggest snowstorm in a quarter century. But that did not deter them – eight hearty souls from Synagogue Lev Chadash who, in the driving snowstorm, accompanied me, their rabbi, to the prison at San Vittore to remember the incarceration of Italian Jews and the murder of the Jews of Europe.

As the snow fell we recalled the horrors of death camp life. One of our group, a young teen, noted that although the snow was deep and the temperature in Milan was below freezing, we Jews were dressed in coats and hats, scarves, gloves, boots and heavy shoes –clothing that the Jews of Auschwitz were so cruelly denied.

In front of the prison, we cleared snow from a park bench to make a place for our candles. Our ceremony included the lighting of six candles to represent the Six Million and to recall the significance of "*Zachor,*" the Hebrew word which means "remember."

"*Zachor*," we said, in voices loud enough for passersby to hear and for some of them to pause and listen. The first candle, recalled "*Shabbat Zachor*" when we hear the story of Amalek and we remember as well that Haman was a direct descendant of one of the first men who set out to kill the Jews. The first candle served as a reminder that evil still exists in our world.

"*Zachor*," we said to candles two and three. Additional definitions of *Zachor* include "to mention," and "to articulate." We remember to speak about those we lost and to tell their stories, like our own Becky Behar Ottolenghi, now of blessed memory, a survivor of the Jewish massacre at Meina (near Lake Como) whose tireless efforts at sharing her experiences with school children earned her Honorary Citizenship from cities all over Italy.

Zachor also asks that we remember those with disabilities and differences. Our fourth candle recalled all of those who, along with the Jews, were also killed, including homosexuals, gypsies, disabled persons and political prisoners.

As the candles struggled and hissed in the falling snow, the *Zachor* of candle five recalled the murdered children. We honored the Holocaust survivors who frequented our synagogue and we paused to honor our own child survivor, Fernanda Diaz, who was saved from certain death by a righteous gentile, an Italian *pescatore* – a simple working man who, when he saw Nazi soldiers approaching, shoved little Fernanda through a trap door in the floor of his fish market. At night he led her to safety, saving her life. We pondered a horrific statistic; that for every Jewish child that lived through the Holocaust, thirteen Jewish children were murdered by the Nazis.

The sixth candle is the *Zachor* of Shabbat. We are reminded that the first strand in the braided *challah*, the bread of the Sabbath, is called *Zachor*. "Remember Shabbat and keep it holy," Torah tells us. And no matter what our trials have been or will be, Shabbat brings us peace, hope and joy.

Later on as we sipped cappuccino in a nearby bar, we learned that in the early morning, just hours before our ceremony, former German President Johannes Rau had passed away. He was the first person to speak in the German language in the halls of the Israeli Knesset. The mission of Rau's presidency was to improve German –Israeli relations by first seeking forgiveness for the Holocaust.

He told the Israel Parliament, "...I bow in humility before those murdered and ... I am asking forgiveness for what Germans have done."

Sadly international news services hardly mentioned President Rau's death that day, in part because the news was dominated by events in the Middle East. On that January 27, Europe was reeling. Hamas was officially designated the winner of the Palestinian elections. This prompted journalists all over Europe to ask how we Jews felt about the upset victory by an organization that vowed to destroy the State of Israel.

As we readied ourselves to brave the cold, the bar's television set blared overhead. Mittens and scarves in hand, we stopped to watch as a sprightly BBC journalist asked an Auschwitz survivor, "Just what lesson did you learn from your experiences?" Without missing a beat, the elderly gentleman pulled the microphone close and said, "Dahling, this I learned. If someone says he wants to kill you, believe him."

Our ceremony of remembrance on January 27, 2006 in Milan was a day filled with contrasts. Leaving the warmth of the bar behind us, we visited our candles once more. As they flickered in the snow we offered the Kaddish Memorial prayer and ended with the words of Psalm 133. *Hinei MaTov,* "How good and pleasant it is when we dwell together as brothers and sisters."

We joined hands, sang and promised to remember *Zachor.*

About Rabbi Barbara Aiello

Rabbi Barbara Aiello is the first woman rabbi and first non-orthodox rabbi in Italy. Following her rabbinate at Italy's first modern liberal synagogue in Milan, she returned to her ancestral home in the deep south of Italy to found Sinagoga Ner Tamid del Sud, the first active synagogue in Calabria in 500 years where she has served since 2006. She is the founder of the B'nei Anusim movement of southern Italy.

Rabbi Aiello has lectured internationally and written extensively about her crypto-Jewish background and her efforts to uncover the hidden Jewish traditions of Calabria Jews that date back to Inquisition times. She has shared her story as scholar-in-residence at synagogues and community centers from Boston to Los Angeles to Winnipeg and Toronto. In 2015 her work was featured in a documentary film, "The Secret Jews of Calabria", which premiered at the historic Brotherhood Synagogue in New York City.

As a *"bat anusim"*, Rabbi Aiello shares her personal story of her family's Jewish journey from forced conversion to secret observance. Her work in the deep south of Italy and in Sicily includes directing the Italian Jewish Cultural Center of Calabria (IjCCC), an organization dedicated to the *anusim* of southern Italy to help them discover and embrace their Jewish roots.

In addition, Rabbi Barbara is the host of the Radio Rabbi program, a Jewish radio broadcast dedicated to Jewish pluralism, now in its twelfth year. The Radio Rabbi program is broadcast on WLSS AM 930 in Sarasota, Florida and is heard live stream and podcast around the world at her website: www.rabbibarbara.com

Hadassa Word Press

More **Books!**

yes **I want** morebooks!

Buy your books fast and straightforward online - at one of the world's fastest growing online book stores! Environmentally sound due to Print-on-Demand technologies.

Buy your books online at
www.get-morebooks.com

Kaufen Sie Ihre Bücher schnell und unkompliziert online – auf einer der am schnellsten wachsenden Buchhandelsplattformen weltweit! Dank Print-On-Demand umwelt- und ressourcenschonend produziert.

Bücher schneller online kaufen
www.morebooks.de

OmniScriptum Marketing DEU GmbH
Bahnhofstraße 28
66111 Saarbrücken, Deutschland   info@omniscriptum.com   OMNIScriptum
Telefax: +49 681 37 20 174-9   www.omniscriptum.com

Made in United States
North Haven, CT
08 March 2023

33781506R00049